SHIPWRECKS OF THE BRISTOL CHANNEL

GRAHAM SMITH

COUNTRYSIDE BOOKS
NEWBURY, BERKSHIRE

Also by Graham Smith:
Smuggling in the Bristol Channel 1700–1850

First published 1991
© Graham Smith 1991

COUNTRYSIDE BOOKS
3 Catherine Road
Newbury, Berkshire

ISBN 1 85306 153 0

Front cover illustration: from G. Ramsay's *Shipwrecks and Disasters at Sea*

Produced through MRM Associates Ltd., Reading
Typeset by Acorn Bookwork, Salisbury
Printed in England by J.W. Arrowsmith Ltd., Bristol

For Joan

Acknowledgements

Several people have assisted in the production of this book. My special thanks go to my sister and brother-in-law, Jean and David Prosser, who spent many hours researching in local libraries along the Welsh coast. Also I wish to thank Mr Cedric Howell for his interest and valued comments on the chapter relating to his escapade.

No person writing on shipwrecks in the Bristol Channel can fail to acknowledge the pioneer research and work of the late Grahame Farr; we, later writers, owe him a deep debt of gratitude.

Several museums, institutions, local newspapers and individuals provided illustrations for this book and I thank them for their assistance.

Finally, but not least, this book would not have been completed so speedily without the encouragement and forbearance of my wife, Joan.

Graham Smith
July 1991

Contents

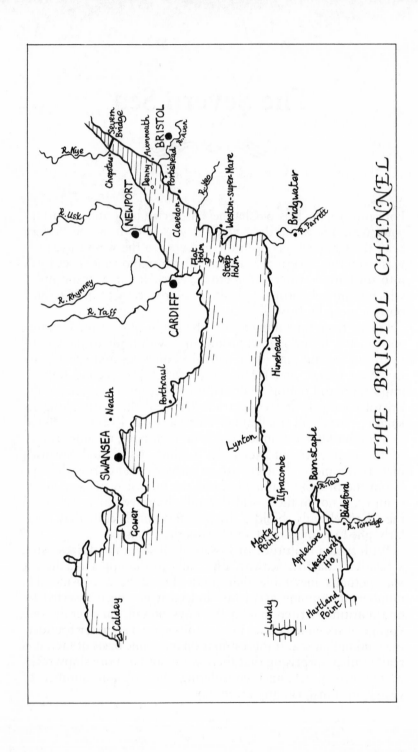

THE BRISTOL CHANNEL

The Severn Sea

For centuries the Bristol Channel has been a busy and important waterway. From the days when it was known as the 'Severn Sea', the Channel has been the gateway to the western seas. It was from this Severn Sea that the first intrepid sailors set forth into uncharted waters in a brave search for new trade links, which ultimately brought wealth and prosperity to the Channel ports, especially Bristol.

Indeed from time immemorial the major port of the Channel was Bristol. It first gained prominence with trade to the Continent and Ireland, and later with the Americas and specifically the West Indies, and for many centuries was second only in importance to London as a port. It fast became the mecca of the Bristol Channel, attracting trade from all the ports along its length – large and small alike. Then, as Bristol's trade suffered as a result of fierce competition from Liverpool, the importance of the coal ports of Newport, Cardiff, Barry and Swansea increased rapidly, their growth so meteoric that during the coal boom the Bristol Channel became the busiest waterway in the country, if not in the world. Literally hundreds of vessels used the Channel daily, besides the countless small craft that regularly plied up and down and across the Channel.

With such a multitude of vessels of all shapes and sizes using a relatively narrow seaway, especially in the upper reaches, it was perhaps inevitable that there should be a considerable number of shipping accidents. Indeed it has been asserted by one maritime writer that in the days of sail, on average one voyage in six ended either in a stranding on a shore or foundering (sinking) at sea. If this estimation has some basis of fact, it is really rather surprising that there were not far more shipwrecks in the Bristol Channel considering the colossal number of vessels in transit on any given day.

The Bristol Channel is not an easy waterway to sail, in fact it is considered particularly dangerous; as one old Channel sailor remarked 'Our Channel is a dreadful place – if you don't know your way around'. The Channel opens out to the full fury of the Atlantic Ocean with its notorious heavy rolling seas, which have gained strength and speed over two and a half thousand unbroken miles from the coast of Newfoundland. The prevailing westerly or south-westerly winds make the Channel a far more difficult waterway to leave than to enter. Out of 100 shipwrecks in the last decades of the 19th century no less than 70 occurred on the outward journey.

Another problem for mariners is that the Channel has one of the highest tidal ranges in the world, which is the actual vertical difference between high and low water. This means that the rate of tidal flow is far higher than normal for the British coast. It is quite usual for the flood tide to flow at three knots increasing to

The French vessel *ACL* which went ashore at Woolacombe Sands in January 1894 and refloated in Ilfracombe Harbour. (Picture: Ilfracombe Museum)

six knots higher up the Channel and the ebb tide runs even stronger. Such fierce tides make the Bristol Channel difficult to negotiate even in good weather but when strengthened by a south-westerly gale they become most formidable. Many stretches of the coast have their own particular dangers with vicious tide races and rips – most notorious are Bideford Bar, Cefn Sidan Sands and the Nash Sands. The vast tidal flow brings masses of mud, sand and sediment down the Channel, which has resulted in a number of dangerous sandbanks creating further hazards to navigation.

The southern coast of the Bristol Channel from Hartland Point to Bridgwater Bay is an almost endless chain of reefs, rocks and daunting vertical cliffs; majestic scenery that attracts the summer visitors but in the winter is a furious coast, often called 'the Cruel Coast' from the number of vessels that have been wrecked along its shores. Hartland Point well deserves its reputation as a lethal place for shipping. In 1852 a traveller described the scene:

'Fragments of rocks everywhere attest the nature of the coast. If an unfortunate vessel is driven by a north-west or a south-west gale within the Horns of Hartland and Padstow Points, God help her hapless crew! for she is doomed to certain destruction. Along the whole coast there is no harbour of refuge – nothing but iron rocks. Here the roar of the ocean is incessant, and in stormy weather appalling. Mighty waves then fling themselves against the giant cliffs, and bursting with thundering crash, send their spray in salt-showers over the land.'

Further up the coast the two headlands of Baggy Point and Morte Point brought disaster to many sailing ships. The dreaded Morte Stone has long been known as the 'Death Stone' from the number of vessels that have been lost rounding the Point. In the winter of 1852 no less than six ships were wrecked at this very spot. And standing out to sea is Lundy Island, the granite sentinel of the Bristol Channel, which has seen a fair measure of ships wrecked along its steep rocky cliffs.

Although the Welsh coast is not quite so fearsome, it has its own notorious 'black spots' – the Gower coast, Sker Point near Porthcawl and Nash Point have proved deadly to many a vessel.

With the prevailing south-westerly or westerly gales the Welsh coast becomes the lee shore, bringing, especially in the days of sail, special navigational problems to prevent vessels being driven ashore. There is no doubt that the Bristol Channel is a most daunting waterway to sail in any conditions but in extreme or severe weather it can become the graveyard of ships and seamen, as the many cemeteries on both sides of the Channel fully attest.

For most of the 18th century there were very few navigational aids for mariners using the Channel. Charts were fairly rudimentary; the *Great Britain Coasting Pilot*, first published by Collins in 1693, was widely used by British seamen throughout the century though it was strongly criticised for its inaccuracies. The first Admiralty charts appeared in 1801 and their now famous *Sailing Directions* were first published in 1828. There were very few lighthouses around the whole of the British coastline and only two in the Bristol Channel – one on Flat Holm erected in 1737 and one at Mumbles Head built in 1794, though the chapel of St Nicholas on Lantern Hill at Ilfracombe had been for centuries a light for Channel sailors. The priests kept a wood fire burning through the winter and it was said to shine like 'a twinkling star'. All of the other famous lighthouses of the Bristol Channel were erected in the 19th century. The first light on Lundy Island appeared in 1820, Braunton in the same year, Burnham's lighthouse-on-legs in 1829 and Nash Point in 1832. The two formidable and dramatic lights on the North Devon coast, Hartland and Bull Points, were built in 1874 and 1879 respectively. The lightships of the Channel – Helwick, Scarweather, Breaksea and the English and Welsh Grounds – all appeared in the 19th century and they quickly became familiar and comforting sights to sailors of all sea-faring nations.

The first organised attempts at life-saving from land fell to the Customs service. In 1815 the Preventive Waterguard was involved in practical experiments with Captain Manby's mortar apparatus. This was basically a strong line attached to a shell which could be fired fairly accurately up to some 275 yards. The idea was to get a line aboard the wrecked vessel in an attempt to rescue the seamen. By 1819 the apparatus was issued to certain preventive stations situated along particularly dangerous stretches of coast. In August 1815 the Collector at Barnstaple

The Rocket Apparatus at work.

was asked whether he could place any of these 'rocket apparatus'. He replied:

'In this port the coast is generally rocky beach and bold shore. There are frequent wrecks, generally close below the cliffs and are very difficult to reach. However, there are two places where the mortars would be of some use, at Mortehoe and Lynmouth but at the port of Ilfracombe what is needed is the provision of a lifeboat'.

Though the apparatus was heavy and cumbersome and not really suited to rocky terrain, all Coastguard stations were supplied with Manby rockets by 1825.

It was in 1823 that Sir William Hillary issued an appeal for a national sea-rescue service:

'. . . From the calamity of shipwreck no one can say that he may at all times remain free; and whilst he is now providing only for the safety of others, a day may come which will render the cause his own.'

Such was the determination and the persuasiveness of his appeal that in the following year the 'National Institution for the

11

Preservation of Life from Shipwreck' was established. The founder's intention was that this unique service would be funded by voluntary donations and subscriptions, which he thought 'would be found easy in its progress and successful in its results'. However, after the initial enthusiasm for the service died down, financial support fell away and by the early 1850s many lifeboats had become run down through lack of funds. During this period of sad decline of the Lifeboat Service, the Customs cutters became increasingly involved in rescues at sea and the Coastguard in life saving from land; though during this period there were very many instances in the Bristol Channel of pilots and local fishermen saving the lives of seamen, and indeed several were awarded cash payments and medals by the Lifeboat Institution.

The honour of the first lifeboat in the Bristol Channel falls to Appledore. In February 1825, less than twelve months after the foundation of the Institution, a boat named the *Volunteer* was supplied, funded by the gentry and merchants in the area. In 1831 a second boat was provided for the station, which ultimately (in 1848) was transferred to the nearby but still remote Braunton Burrows, where a special lifeboat house had been built. Just 13 years after the Customs Collector had recommended a lifeboat for Ilfracombe, the port received its first boat, and a lifeboat was supplied at Burnham on Sea in 1836.

The Welsh coast had only two early lifeboats – one at Laugharne and one at Swansea. The former only lasted a few years and because the boat at Swansea was not considered 'a good sailing boat', the Swansea Harbour Trustees refused to spend much money on it. Indeed the Northumberland report of 1851, which made a survey of the lifeboat service throughout the country, disclosed that 'on the south coast of Wales from Cardiff to Fishguard, a distance of 200 miles, there is one lifeboat at Swansea and that is unserviceable'.

It was largely the fourth Duke of Northumberland and his excellent report that brought about the resuscitation of the Institution's fortunes. In 1851 he became its President, three years later the name was changed to the Royal National Lifeboat Institution and since then it has gone from strength to strength. In the year he became President, the Duke launched his now famous competition for an efficient, effective and safe lifeboat design. The winner of this competition was James Beeching, whose design was for a 36 ft boat capable of carrying about 70 people and with a self-righting capability. Beeching's basic lifeboat design would last for many years.

The 1860s saw a considerable upsurge of the Lifeboat Service in the Bristol Channel. Lifeboat stations were established at Ferryside, Porthcawl, Penarth, Pembrey, Lynmouth and Clovelly, and in 1866 the Swansea boat was moved to the now famous Mumbles station. By the end of the century there were lifeboat stations also at Watchet, Morte Bay, Port Eynon, Weston-super-Mare and, one year later (1901), at Barry and Minehead. There was no doubt that at this time the coasts of the Bristol Channel were very comprehensively covered by lifeboats.

One of the features of the latter decades of the 19th century was the formation of many local Lifesaving Apparatus Companies (LSA). These companies were manned solely by local volunteers and they owe their origin to the days when the Coastguard were forced to request the help of local people to handle their rocket apparatus. The Manby rocket had now been superseded by a more efficient and lighter apparatus designed by a Captain Boxer and named after him. This reliable system was in use well into the 20th century and the various LSA companies were responsible for the saving of many lives. In the Bristol Channel there were LSA companies at Clovelly, Westward Ho, Croyde, Ilfracombe, Lynmouth, Hartland Quay, Lundy, Mortehoe and on the Welsh coast at Rhossili, Horton, Port Talbot and Porthcawl.

There have been many brave and thrilling rescues by lifeboats stationed in the Bristol Channel, some of which appear later in this book. The Royal National Lifeboat Institution is a unique service, completely supported by voluntary subscriptions. Each lifeboat station is administered by its own locally elected committee and the lifeboats are manned by volunteer seamen of a very high quality, who through the years have shown such dedication and bravery in the saving of hundreds of lives. The current lifeboats in use were all designed at the Institution's headquarters at Poole in Dorset. Nowadays the 'Fleet' comprises a variety of types and sizes of vessels from the largest – the 70 ft 'Clyde' to the small and fast inflatable boats. The

Prototype of the R.N.L.I.'s lifeboat undergoing sea trials in the Solent in 1991.
(Picture: Peter Orme)

Institution is always searching for improvements in lifeboat design and very recently a new lifeboat underwent trials in the Solent. At the time of writing there are lifeboat stations at Appledore, Ilfracombe, Barry, Mumbles and Tenby, with smaller boats at Weston-super-Mare, Minehead, Penarth, St Donats, Porthcawl, Horton, Port Eynon and Burry Port. The Lifeboat Service has a long and proud history of life-saving at sea and the various Bristol Channel lifeboats have made ample contribution to this fine and courageous tradition.

As an introduction to the drama and tragedy of shipwrecks in the Bristol Channel it is perhaps fitting to quote a writer who more than any other is part of the Bristol Channel scene – Charles Kingsley. From 1831 to 1836 Charles Kingsley's father was curate at Clovelly and one of the most indelible family memories of that place was of a wrecked ship being pounded by mountainous seas. Every one of the writing Kingsleys – Charles, Charlotte and Henry – used the incident in their novels. Charles first described it in 1849:

'... in the roaring December morning, we watched from the Hartland Cliffs a great barque, which came drifting and rolling in before the western gale, while we followed her up the coast, parsons and sportsmen, farmers and preventive men, with the Manby motor lumbering behind us in a cart, through stone gaps and track-ways, from headland to headland – The maddening excitement of sheer expectation as she ran wildly towards the cliffs at our feet, and then sheered off again inexplicably ...
Well I recollect the mingled disappointment of the preventive men, as a fresh set of survivors appeared in view, in the form of a boat's crew of Clovelly fishermen ... And how they tried to get her head round to the wind, and disappeared instantly in a cloud of white spray – and let her head fall back again – and jammed it round again, and disappeared again – and at last let her drive helplessly up the bay, while we kept pace with her along the cliffs ... how she broke loose from them at the last moment and [eventually at Mouth Mill – some two miles north-west of Clovelly] she rushed frantically in upon those rocks below us, leaping great banks of slate at the blow of each breaker tearing off masses of ironstone which lie there to this very day to tell the tale, till she drove up high and dry against the cliff, and lay, like an enormous stranded whale, grinding and crashing herself to pieces against the walls of her adamantine cage ...'

One Green Bottle

In 1957 a small green bottle was washed ashore at Portledge Mouth, a delightful little beach which nestles between the red cliffs of Babbacombe and Peppercombe with splendid views across the Bristol Channel to Lundy Island in the distance.

The small bottle looked quite old, perhaps Victorian, and on close inspection seemed to be perfectly sealed. When it was opened, it was found to contain a letter, which fortunately had been unaffected by water. The letter read:

> '15th August 1843
>
> Dear Brother
>
> Please e God I be with y against Michaelmas.
> Prepare y search Lundy for y Jenny ivories.
> Adiue William Odessa'

On the reverse of the letter was a roughly drawn map of Lundy Island with a cross in the centre of the west coast, presumably to mark where the 'Jenny Ivories' were to be found.

It is amazing and quite inexplicable how this old bottle, so perfectly preserved, had managed to survive 114 years of washing around the Bristol Channel. Nevertheless its discovery and the letter it contained linked two shipwrecks in the Channel, the earliest having occurred no less than 160 years previously.

From the few positive leads in the brief letter, considerable research was required before it was determined that it had been written by a seaman serving on a brig called the *Caledonia*. Furthermore it was thought to have been destined for his brother who lived in the West Country and it seems most likely that the bottle was thrown overboard whilst the vessel was travelling along the north Cornwall coast.

The *Caledonia* was a 200 ton brig from Arbroath in Scotland. She had loaded coffee in Rio de Janiero for the ports of Syria, Smyrna and Constantinople. From Turkey she passed into the Black Sea to load wheat at Odessa (where the letter was written) for ultimate discharge at Gloucester. By 5th September 1843 the vessel had arrived at Falmouth Roads; from there she proceeded on the last leg of her voyage along the Cornwall coast before entering the Bristol Channel.

For the first day or so the sailing conditions remained good, at least until the evening of 7th September when the weather suddenly worsened from the north-west – a most dangerous quarter when sailing along the north Cornwall and Devon coasts. By just after midnight there was a very strong north-north-west gale blowing, which increased steadily in severity as the night wore on. The master of the vessel, Captain Peter, tried to keep her on course but despite his and the crew's efforts the *Caledonia* was being inexorably driven closer and closer to the leeside shore. At about three o'clock in the morning she struck rocks at Vicarage Cliffs, Morwenstow, on the border between Cornwall and Devon.

The captain immediately ordered his men up into the main rigging but, unfortunately, within several minutes the vessel was subjected to some particularly heavy seas, which not only submerged her but brought the main mast crashing down and all the crew were thrown into the sea. Only one member of the crew survived – Edward La Daine, a Channel Islander; he was thrust onto the reef and with a superhuman effort managed to drag himself painfully across the razor-sharp rocks until he was high enough out of the water to be safe. La Daine collapsed from exhaustion and remained unconscious for several hours.

A young farm boy had seen the tangled remains of the battered ship from the top of the cliffs. He climbed down for a closer look to see whether there was anything of value he could pick up, and it was only then that he discovered the body of the unconscious seaman. La Daine was fortunate in at least two respects – not only that he survived, but also that he should be cast upon that particular stretch of coast which came within the parish of Morwenstow and its rather eccentric vicar – the Rev R. S. Hawker.

The Rev Hawker has become one of the real characters of that coast, his odd behaviour and eccentricities having passed into the folk-lore of the area. When he arrived at the parish in 1834 he found the church in a sad state of repair, and he also claimed that the vicarage was being used as a store for smuggled goods and his poor parishioners were a fine mixture of 'smugglers, wreckers and dissenters of various hues'. Nevertheless he soon brought some conformity to the parish and quickly became enchanted by the rugged splendour of the coast. He even built a small hut out of shipwreck timber high up on the cliffs to overlook the magnificent scenery. It was in this rude hut that he did much of his writing, for which he is now famed. Though few of his stories can be backed up by hard facts, he embroidered some quite frightening tales of smuggling and wrecking life along that part of the coast.

To his eternal credit the Rev Hawker instigated a reward system for those of his parishioners who aided shipwrecked sailors and even for those who managed to recover bodies. Later he was very proud to recall that between 30 and 40 shipwrecked seamen had been given a Christian burial in his churchyard. La Daine was therefore brought to Hawker, who cared for him in the rectory and, as he recuperated, so the story of the shipwreck unfolded.

La Daine maintained that the *Caledonia* was an 'unlucky' ship. She had sailed from Rio on a Friday, the Argentinian cook had come aboard with a black bag and furthermore during the voyage he had lost a bucket overboard – all three incidents were thought unlucky by sailors in the early 19th century. During the vessel's stay in Constantinople the cook had become involved in a brawl at an inn and received a knife wound, which worsened on the passage back to England. Finally the cook died and was buried at sea – another ill-omen according to La Daine. Despite all this he stoutly maintained that the captain bore no responsibility for the wreck, he considered him a splendid seaman with a long experience of sailing the world. It would seem that the cabin boy, a poor lad of twelve years, was to blame. He had broken the tube of the barometer at Falmouth and thus the captain had no advance warning of the impending storm!

The bottle, containing a letter from a sailor to his brother, which survived 114 years in the Bristol Channel before it was finally found. (Picture: The Portledge Hotel)

Within a day or so all the bodies of the drowned crew were washed up and recovered and they were buried in the churchyard at Morwenstow. The Rev Hawker even wrote a short poem about the sad ceremony:

> 'We laid them in their lowly rest,
> The strangers from a distant shore:-
> We smoothed the green turf on their breast,
> Mid baffled ocean's angry roar!
> And there – the relique of the storm –
> We fixed fair Scotland's figured form.'

The 'relique' was the figurehead of the brig, which is still preserved in the churchyard over 150 years later; as indeed is Hawker's little hut perched perilously some 400 ft above the spot where the *Caledonia* finally sunk. The hut is now maintained by the National Trust and is along the route of the Somerset and North Devon Coast Path.

So William, the writer of the letter in the green bottle, lies in Morwenstow churchyard. The *Jenny* he had referred to was a three-masted schooner, which on 20th February 1797 was homeward bound to Bristol from Africa with a cargo of ivory and gold dust. As she battled up the Bristol Channel in a terrific storm she was driven onto the rocks on the west side of the island – this was before there were any lighthouses on Lundy. The place where the vessel was wrecked has been known ever since as Jenny's Cove. All the crew perished and very soon all signs of the wreck disappeared. The ivory was recovered some few years later but the leather bags containing the gold were never found. So even had poor William survived the wreck of the *Caledonia*, the chances of he and his brother striking it rich would have been very slim indeed.

The small green bottle and the letter are now on display at the Portledge Hotel, a splendid 17th century mansion, set in about 1,000 acres of park and farmland at Fairy Cross, some four miles along the Clovelly road from Bideford.

Lucky To Be Alive

On Saturday 29th August 1908 the morning shift at Roath
Dock, Cardiff had just completed loading the *Verajean* with
over 3,000 tons of patent fuel for Chile. The three-masted steel
sailing vessel was relatively new, built in Dumbarton, Scotland
in 1891 and the flagship of the Verajean Shipping Company.
She had spent some considerable time in Roath Dock as she had
arrived from Chile nearly one month earlier with a full cargo of
ore. Her master, Captain Ritchie, was justifiably proud of his
vessel: at 1,933 tons she was quite large, by contemporary
standards, and her all steel construction gave her a speed
advantage over similar sized iron-clad vessels.

The captain was eager to leave. He was very loath to spend
another weekend in port, where the dock charges were high to
pay for the most modern quay facilities – after all, the Roath
Dock had only been opened some 21 years earlier. Furthermore
a vessel in port did not create income, in fact rather the
contrary, and the captain's performance was largely judged by
the profitability of each voyage. Thus Captain Ritchie was
under certain pressure to sail when it would have been wiser to
stay in port. Despite the fact that the barometer was rapidly
falling and that severe summer storms in late August were not
unknown to the Bristol Channel, the captain ordered two tugs
for the evening tide.

At nine p.m. on Saturday evening the *Verajean* left Cardiff
with the assistance of the two tugs the *Lady Morgan* and the
Salvor, but they had barely rounded Penarth Head before
Captain Ritchie realised that the wind strength had suddenly
increased. It was later said to be a force eight (near gale) and
gusting to force nine (strong gale). In the circumstances Captain
Ritchie decided to hove-to in Barry Roads – a relatively shel-

A postcard of the wreck of the *Verajean*, August 1908. She stayed marooned for days on the rocks at Rhoose Point, finally deemed fit only for salvage. (Picture: Glamorgan Record Office)

tered anchorage – until the morning to see whether the conditions improved.

Sunday morning broke with no improvement in the weather, nor indeed any appreciable deterioration, so the captain decided to carry on down the Channel. Even with the assistance of the two tugs it was a battle against a ferocious south-westerly gale. It took over 24 hours just to reach the vicinity of Lundy Island. At one p.m. on the Monday, the first tug, the *Lady Morgan*, released its tow followed shortly after by the *Salvor* and both tugs made for the shelter of Lundy Roads. The two masters later claimed that the severity of the weather was such that they were in fear of colliding and in any case they had only agreed to tow the vessel out of the Bristol Channel and Lundy had long been considered the limit of the Channel. Captain Ritchie stoutly maintained that he had expected the tow to continue further westward until *he* decided that their services were no longer needed.

Whatever the rights in the affair, the tugs had departed and the captain was faced with a dilemma. Should he attempt to progress further out into the full force of the Atlantic or should he seek shelter? The barometer was still falling and there was no sign of the atrocious weather abating. He now considered the conditions so bad that he decided to beat back up the Channel to Barry Roads. He discounted nearby Lundy in the belief that it was a most dangerous and treacherous coast and ill-suited to a vessel of the *Verajean's* size. Later some more experienced Bristol Channel sailors voiced the opinion that this decision was flawed, but, of course, that was with the great benefit of hindsight.

It must be remembered that ships were built to stand almost any weather and had to survive all kinds of storms, though it did require good seamanship and long experience to ride out a storm. Indeed very few vessels were lost purely through severe weather *alone*, always providing the master had sufficient sea-room, which was rarely the case in a relatively narrow and confined seaway like the Bristol Channel. So on balance Captain Ritchie felt that he had made the right decision in the circumstances.

He set the minimum amount of canvas to give the vessel steerage and as they would now be sailing before the wind, they would be driven in a north-easterly direction across the Channel. By eleven p.m. on Monday evening they were off Swansea Bay; the *Verajean* had crossed the Bristol Channel at virtually its widest point. The captain's problem now was to prevent his vessel being driven ashore. Four hours later they were close to Nash Point and another half an hour saw them abreast of the Breaksea lightship, which marked the entrance to Barry Roads. Captain Ritchie must have breathed a long sigh of relief. He had managed to bring the *Verajean* along a most dangerous coast in very severe conditions and had successfully negotiated such notorious spots as Mumbles Head, Sker Rock, Tusker and Nash Sands and Nash Point.

It was now four o'clock in the morning of Tuesday and the captain decided to hove-to and ride out the storm. After all it had been raging for well over two days so there was every reasonable chance that it would soon blow itself out. Little did he know that within the next few hours it would reach its most destructive height. He gave the order to drop anchor and, although the vessel was thought to be in eleven fathoms of water, the starboard anchor chain was run out to its very end and it and its securings disappeared into the angry sea. The same thing happened with the port anchor, so now the *Verajean* was almost completely at the mercy of the storm. One of the crew later described the situation as like being 'a cork in the midst of boiling water'. Captain Ritchie attempted to get some canvas on the foremast but they were ripped away in a terrific gust of wind – it was described as 'blowing like a hurricane'.

Captain Ritchie now realised that despite all his and the crew's endeavours, their long battle with the storm had ended, his ship was lost. He gave the order to abandon ship and within minutes of the boats getting away, the *Verajean* was dashed onto rocks at Rhoose Point, the most southerly point of Wales and less than a mile or so from Barry Roads – so near and yet so far! Almost as soon as the ship grounded the main topmast split and fell and the *Verajean* settled down at an angle of 45° barely 200 yards from the shore.

Mercifully all the crew and the captain managed to reach the shore despite the tremendous seas. One eye-witness on the shore said 'It was incredible that the boats did not overturn as there were massive waves battering the rocks and yet not one man was drowned – it was beyond belief!' The captain's first comments on reaching land were said to be 'Thank God, we are lucky to be alive!' Later on and after due reflection he would consider himself and his crew as very lucky indeed, when the full details of the ferocity of the storm became known. It has passed into the weather folk-lore of the Bristol Channel as 'The Great Hurricane of 1908'. Considerable damage was done on land, especially along the Glamorgan coast, which seemed to bear the brunt of the storm. Considering that the *Verajean* had sailed down to Lundy Island and back through such severe weather, it was a miracle that no lives were lost.

The poor vessel stayed firmly marooned for the next ten days, although by Tuesday evening the worst of the storm had passed. For that time she proved to be a great spectacle for the locals and even special trips from Cardiff were arranged to view the wreck. Some enterprising photographer managed to get a good shot of the vessel and it was used on special postcards. The

The figurehead of the iron ship *Amazon* wrecked on Margam Sands in the ferocious storm of 1908. (Picture: National Maritime Museum)

Verajean was finally towed away to Barry Docks for repairs but was holed so badly that she was fit only for salvage. At the end of the year she was towed back along the Glamorgan coast to a breaker's yard; a rather sad and inglorious end for a vessel that had suffered so much at the hands of the storm.

The Court of Enquiry into the wreck reported in November of the same year. It exonerated the masters of the two tugs who, it was felt, had been fully justified in their actions. The Court also considered that Captain Ritchie had done all that was humanly possible to save his ship and crew.

Other vessels caught in the Great Hurricane were not so lucky. The *Amazon* left Port Talbot early on Monday morning, also loaded with coal for Chile. Assisted by tugs, she managed to struggle as far as Mumbles Point. The master, Captain Garrack, decided to anchor in the Outer Roads for the night. By early the following morning the anchors could no longer hold the heavily loaded ship in such adverse conditions. The *Amazon* was inexorably pushed back down the coast and by eight a.m. (just an hour or so after the *Verajean* struck the rocks) she was driven ashore at Margam Sands, very close to the entrance of Port Talbot harbour.

It was a terrifying scene of death and destruction as the mountainous seas crashed over the decks. The vessel's lifeboat was destroyed just when it was being launched. Some of the crew were flung into the water by the force of the waves and those clinging to the masts were propelled into the sea as one by one the masts collapsed. Only six of the crew managed to make it to the shore and one of these died two days later in hospital. After about an hour and a half a rescue party was able to get on board but by this time there were only two survivors left – the first mate and a seaman. Out of a total crew of 28 there were only eight survivors. Captain Garrack's body was not found for eight days; it was recovered at Sker Point – another notorious place for wrecks. The *Amazon* is still remembered in Port Talbot to this day and is commemorated by the Amazon public house in an area of the town close to the scene of the wreck.

A Sad Mishap

By the middle of the Victorian age Weston-super-Mare had become a most popular seaside resort attracting thousands of 'excursionists' every bank holiday. Many of these came by train from Bristol but after the opening of the Birnbeck pier in 1867 many more came by sea. The new pier afforded a deep-water anchorage at all states of the tide and the resort was opened up to the heavily populated Welsh towns across the Channel. Weston-super-Mare became the place to visit for a day at the seaside with the added bonus of a pleasant and healthy trip across the briny.

On 22nd September 1884 one such excursion had left Bristol early for a day's trip to Weston but because it was late summer there were only 42 passengers on board. Each had paid one shilling and sixpence for their return ticket. The vessel was the *Welsh Prince*, a little 118 ton steamer with auxiliary staysails; she was normally used on more mundane duties, ferrying goods and passengers from Newport to Bristol. On this day the passengers had about five hours to sample and enjoy the delights of Weston before returning in the early evening. Usually the arrival and departure of these small passenger steamers created great interest with the holidaymakers. Crowds gathered along the pier (admission twopence) for a breath of fresh sea air, a look at the maritime activity and then a gentle stroll back to their hotel or guest house in time for dinner – a typical Victorian seaside scene.

It was no different on this late summer evening. According to reports, 'the pier was thronged with people though there was a brisk wind blowing with a touch of autumn in the air'. Six o'clock was the departure time of the *Welsh Prince* and once all the passengers were safely on board, the whole rigmarole of

The *Welsh Prince* seen here loading cargo near Newport Bridge, caused great excitement in 1884 when she ran into trouble whilst on a holiday excursion to Weston-super-Mare. (Picture: The Collection of Newport Museum and Art Gallery)

casting off was commenced with some arcane directions being shouted from the master to the pier attendants, which created much interest and great amusement. By all accounts Captain Rowe of the *Welsh Prince* was always ready to 'play to the gallery' and make the departure appear a much more involved procedure than it really was!

On this evening though the operation went sadly wrong. Just as the last mooring rope was being cast off, it wound itself around the vessel's propeller and because of 'the rough sea and the strong north-westerly wind' she was quickly driven into Sand Bay, just to the north-east of the pier. The captain and the engineer wrestled with the engine in a vain attempt to clear the rope either by shaking it off or snapping it. As the vessel was drifting perilously close inshore, Captain Rowe dropped the anchors, hoisted distress flats and sounded the ship's whistle furiously for help.

This created great excitement amongst the spectators on the pier and very shortly they were to get added value for their two pennies. The urgent distress whistles had brought out the lifeboatmen. The lifeboat, which was called the *William James Holt*, had only been established just over two years and this was to be their first real-life rescue bid. The lifeboat was slung from davits hanging on the north side of the pier. Within a half an hour the boat was manned and the crowd were treated to a rather spectacular launching. The lifeboat was, of course, propelled by oars and by all accounts the crew were encouraged and cheered every stroke of the way!

Meanwhile back on the *Welsh Prince* the situation had become rather tense. The anchors were dragging and the vessel seemed in very real danger of grounding. Several of the passengers had to be physically restrained from jumping into the sea to take their chance on swimming ashore. The crew tried to bolster up the courage of some of the passengers, many of whom were in a distressed state. However, within 15 minutes the lifeboat was alongside and the first 20 passengers were taken off. The children were thrown down into the waiting arms of the lifeboatmen and two persons had to be dragged out of the sea because they misjudged the movement of the boat. Soon the lifeboat was making its way back with the first survivors and this proved a more difficult task as they were rowing against a strong head wind and a rough sea. On the second trip all the passengers were recovered and there was not a single injury. The captain and his crew refused to leave as they felt that she would go aground on the sand without any great danger.

One of the spectators on the pier said that there appeared to be no panic on the vessel, though he could clearly hear some of the ladies crying out for help and when the passengers were landed safely on the pier many could be heard 'loudly proclaiming their thanks to God for their safe deliverance'. There was universal praise for the lifeboat crew and the *Weston Gazette* commented that 'A Great Tragedy had been averted by the speed and bravery of their actions'. The editor speculated on how fortunate it had been for the passengers that the lifeboat had at last been established in the town 'due to the munificence of Colonel Holt of Bangor'. Captain Rowe was asked, 'Whether he felt there was any danger to the passengers and whether he thought at any time that his vessel would be wrecked?' His reply was very clear 'Never, t'was nothing more than a sad mishap. She'll weather all that this sea can throw at her!'

Eventually the *Welsh Prince* was stranded high and dry on the sands – the tide does go out a rather long distance at Weston as any holidaymaker can confirm! This enabled the offending rope and hawser to be cut away and she was refloated on the next tide with virtually no damage suffered. Some of the passengers were offered free accommodation for the night but most returned to Bristol by train. It had proved to be a more exciting and prolonged excursion than they had expected.

The *Welsh Prince* was probably the most famous of all cross-Channel boats. From 1871 to 1886 she was one of the major links between South Wales and Bristol. Indeed in 1874 she did no less than 160 trips across the Channel as well as numerous summer excursions. The opening of the Severn railway tunnel in 1886 rather restricted her usefulness but she continued to sail the Channel as a collier until 1930 when she was broken up. Her captain, William Rowe, was considered to be 'one of the most colourful personalities in the Bristol Channel'.

Heroes or Sharks?

Shipwrecks leave an indelible mark on the history of a locality. The stories of terrible storms and tragic shipping disasters live on and are handed down from generation to generation. For those who live by the coast and more so for those who gain their livelihood from the sea, these stories are a constant reminder of the awesome powers of the elements and the inherent risks incurred in not giving due respect to such potent forces. Nevertheless, it is indeed rare to find a strong and heated debate still being conducted about a shipwreck that had occurred over 100 years earlier, as was the case in Ilfracombe in 1904.

The facts of the shipwreck, at least as far as they can be ascertained at this distance in time, are that a convoy of vessels from the West Indies bound for Bristol were battling their way through storms in the approaches to the Bristol Channel during the early days of October 1796. The gales, which had raged incessantly for well over a week, had scattered the ships; one, the *Ann Mary*, was stranded on the Irish coast near Kinsale and another, the *Fame*, finally found shelter in Rush Bay some miles north of Dublin. The *New Adventure* had managed to stay more on course and despite severe damage to her rigging was making for Ilfracombe to seek shelter – the port had for centuries been used as a haven. She was finally brought safely into the harbour by the hobblers, a local term for boatmen who helped vessels in and out of the port, either by towing or by the use of ropes from the shore.

Some 24 hours later, during the evening of 9th October, another straggler from the convoy, the *London* was also trying to make for Ilfracombe harbour but the gale had increased in ferocity and so much of her rigging was damaged that she was virtually out of steerage, being driven along at the whim of the

Painting of Ilfracombe Harbour in 1796, with the wreck of *London* on the far right hand side. (Picture: Ilfracombe Museum)

storm. Unfortunately she failed to make the entrance of the harbour – the old pier said to date from the 14th century – and was finally driven on to rocks at Rapparee Cove, so very close to the town.

The *London* was a transport vessel under contract to the Government and had on board a considerable number of French prisoners of war and their military guards as well as an unspecified quantity of 'treasure'. Many of the crew and the prisoners were washed overboard, where most drowned or were battered to death on the rocks. Local boats put out in an attempt to save lives and many of the townsmen lined the shore to pull out the few survivors who had managed to escape the tangled mass of timber, spars and rigging. By the following morning 30 bodies had been recovered, of this number no less than 16 were identified as Ilfracombe men, who had drowned in their attempts to save the lives of the crew and prisoners. It was not recorded how many persons were on the vessel or even how many lives were saved.

The Customs Collector at the port makes only brief reference to the incident in his report to London: 'On the 9th inst a transport *London* from St Kitts with French prisoners foundered near this town with great loss of life, we are not aware of any goods carried by this vessel though our present information is that it was only a transport vessel'. Another contemporary record of the wreck was given by the *Exeter Flying Post*:

'On Sunday evening a very melancholy accident happened at Ilfracombe, a ship called the *London* of London from St Kitts, having on board a considerable number of blacks [French prisoners] was driven on the rocks, near the entrance to the pier during a violent gale of wind, by which about fifty of the prisoners were drowned; those who got on shore exhibited a most wretched spectacle, and the scene altogether was too shocking for description. It is reported that the accident was owing to the unskilfulness of the pilot, as the wind was blowing directly fair for the harbour, and if so, it is an additional instance to the many, which have already occurred of the propriety, and absolute necessity of that class of people being registered at every sea-port in the kingdom . . .'

The editor appeared to be parading a personal bete noire – inefficient pilots. The Bristol Channel had a well regulated and organised pilotage system, which had been in operation since the early 17th century. Nevertheless the scapegoat for this tragic shipwreck was the Ilfracombe pilot – the first slur on the conduct of Ilfracombe people concerning this wreck, which would later flare up into a controversy. There is no other evidence that there was a pilot on board the *London* and if the weather conditions were as bad as reported it is most unlikely that any local boat could have reached the *London*. The only other contemporary report appeared in a London journal and this gave the bare facts with no mention of a pilot, indeed it implied that the severe storm was the sole reason for the accident, when 'at least 75 persons were drowned'.

Then in October 1904, 108 years later, an article was published in the *Ilfracombe Parish Magazine* which gave a completely different story of the fate of the survivors of the *London*. This writer quoted a letter said to have been written to the *Illustrated London News* back in 1856:

> 'It is well-known to many old men now living that about 60 years ago, a vessel manned by blacks ran ashore, and that the then best families in the town being nothing but wreckers and smugglers, murdered the crew and buried their bodies on the beach, and then plundered the vessel of a very sizeable cargo, consisting ivory, doubloons, jewels etc. This having caused some disturbance, put an end to the system ... The people here still retain the name of 'Combe Sharks', which appellation was bestowed on them by the surrounding neighbourhood about a century ago [1750s].'

Quite understandably this article incensed many Ilfracombe residents and a furious debate ensued, which culminated in a letter to the local paper in which the writer maintained that according to a 'surviving witness' the local people had done everything possible to save the lives of the crew and the passengers, and upwards of 16 locals had died in the attempt. As for plundering the cargo, the 'treasure' was said to have been contained in five boxes – mainly dollars, doubloons and other coins – one box was reported to have been lost 'in transit from the ship and had probably broken up on the bottom of the sea because dollars and doubloons continued to be found in the sand years after the ship had been lost.'

So now there are two conflicting versions of what happened in the aftermath of the shipwreck. The wrecking story seems unlikely as there is no mention of this in the Customs records of the time, nor indeed any report of cargo being stolen. The absence of any comments is significant as the Collector had previously reported instances of the plunder of wrecked cargo and he was responsible for the security of all such goods. Furthermore the Custom House was then situated on the quay in Ilfracombe and was virtually in sight of the *London* and surely the Customs officers from the port would have been detailed to guard the wreck.

There is at least one plausible explanation for the second version of the story. Perhaps the writer in 1856 was really referring to an earlier wreck, which also became stranded close to Ilfracombe. This was the Portuguese *Nostra Seignora de Bon Succeso*, which was bound for Bristol laden with cargo and was wrecked in October (the same month) but 16 years earlier – in 1780. This vessel would have been 'manned by blacks', at least in the view of the locals any dark-skinned seaman may have been thought of as 'black'. Furthermore she would be more likely to be carrying the cargo mentioned in the letter, 'ivory, doubloons and jewels etc'. However, such conjecture does not completely exculpate Ilfracombe; all that can be said with any certainty is that the *London* was a tragic wreck with a fearful loss of life, which would have been a far greater disaster but for the bravery and sacrifice of the men from Ilfracombe.

To Feed The Hungry And Clothe The Poor

1843 was a disastrous year for shipping in the Bristol Channel. There was a succession of violent storms, which took a heavy toll of both shipping and seamen. These periods of exceptional weather were so uncommon that even the London journals reported the extensive damage done both at land and at sea. The storms were extraordinary in several respects. Their duration was invariably prolonged, some raging for ten days or more, most came with little warning save a sudden and dramatic drop in barometric pressure, but perhaps the most unusual feature was that the majority blew from the north-east quarter rather than the prevailing south-west. As a consequence the north coasts of Cornwall and Devon took the brunt of the shipping casualties whereas the Welsh coast was virtually free of wrecks during the whole year – a rare occurrence.

February, April, September and October all had periods of heavy gales but the middle weeks of January saw a period of unrelenting and extreme weather – at times hurricane-force winds, torrential rain and blizzards. The first shipping victims of these great storms occurred on the north Cornwall coast – a schooner *Hester* from Cork was wrecked at Cape Cornwall though all the crew were rescued by lifeboat. On the same day (10th), a St Ives schooner was sighted off Morwenstow cliffs with only her topmasts showing above the sea and some of her crew clinging to the rigging. The vessel soon disappeared with a complete loss of life. Also on the same day another St Ives schooner, *The Brothers*, was homeward bound from Cardiff with a cargo of coal and was last seen just off Hartland Point on the north Devon coast. She too disappeared with no survivors.

However, perhaps the most famous wreck of this destructive storm was the *John Lilley*, a Liverpool barque that was grounded at the northern end of Saunton Sands just across the Bar from Northam. This vessel came to grief in the early hours of 15th January. She had left Liverpool some two weeks earlier bound for Old Calabar on the west coast of Africa with a full range of 'barter' goods – rum, beads, firearms, cutlery, pots and pans and cotton goods. The first few days were plain sailing but then the weather quickly worsened and for the next ten days Captain Townes and his crew of 25 were in a continual battle with the elements.

First the vessel was blown well off course down to the north Cornwall coast, then the wind veered a couple of points and the *John Lilley* was driven right across the entrance of the Bristol Channel on to the Welsh coast. From there she was lashed back across the Channel to the north Devon coast – the crew must have felt that they were being cast around like a cork. On the morning of the 14th the rudder broke in particularly heavy seas and later in the day the pumps ceased to function. Captain Townes now knew that virtually all hope of saving his vessel had gone, it just seemed a matter of time and on which particular part of the coast she would strike.

The first hour of daylight on the 15th saw the *John Lilley* a couple of miles north-east of Bideford Bar. She was spotted by Captain Williams on his brig *The Shepherdess*, which was battling to reach her home port of Appledore. The captain could see the great difficulties the stricken vessel was in and without a thought for the safety of his own ship and crew, he managed to come alongside the lee of the *John Lilley* – a feat of rare seamanship in such conditions. However, he was unable to effect a transfer of the crew because of the heavy seas and the fact that most of the crew of the *John Lilley* were drunk. Somehow they had managed to broach the cargo of rum. The poor benighted seamen had presumably given up all hope of being saved and now firmly believed that they and their ship were doomed. Less than two hours after this gallant but abortive rescue attempt the *John Lilley* was finally driven onto Saunton Sands, within about two miles of Braunton lighthouse, which had only been erected in 1820 as a precaution against such disasters.

The Braunton Lighthouse, salvation for master and crew of the wrecked *John Lilley* in 1843. (Picture: North Devon Museum Trust)

The lighthouse keeper, Mr Lamping, along with John Bowden, a Customs officer from Appledore, and aided by another local helper, were soon on the scene and they managed, with some difficulty, to save the master and all the crew – amazingly not a single life was lost. Despite the drunken condition of most of the seamen, they were invited to stay overnight in the keeper's house, which adjoined the lighthouse.

The fame or notoriety of the *John Lilley* stems from the time she was firmly grounded on the sands. Within an hour or so the vessel started to break up and her cargo spilled out and was strewn the whole length of the Sands – some three miles in length. The 15th January also happened to fall on a Sunday so all the villagers from nearby Braunton were free from work and thus were able not only to view the dramatic wreck, but also to help themselves to the cargo that was washed up on the beach. The local newspaper reported the scene at the wreck:

'The officers of the revenue, customs and coastguards, were very actively engaged all day on Sunday in superintending the saving of the cargo; and it required their utmost efforts to preserve it from pillage; and but for their timely assistance and resolute defence, most of the property would have found its way across the sandhills . . . The vigilant precautions of the commanding officer of the Customs were barely sufficient to deter the bands of men and women that came down from purloining and carrying away whatever they could lay their hands upon ... It is with some indignation we record to the lasting disgrace of this neighbourhood, that the most bare-faced and shameful robberies have been committed on the wreck ...'

The Customs Collector at Barnstaple was rather more restrained in his report to the Customs Board in London. After reciting the bare facts of the wreck and estimating the value of cargo at about £15,000, he then detailed the steps he had taken to secure the cargo and the wreck. However, he did stress that his officers had done sterling work to try to contain the 'country people' but pointed out that he would have needed 'an army of officers' to deal with such a mammoth task. He did have to admit finally that on the night of the 16th, much cargo disappeared and though searches in the village had been made very few goods had been recovered. The situation was made more difficult by another wrecked vessel, the schooner *Little Test* from Southampton, which had beached a few hours later less than a mile or so from the *John Lilley*. He pointed out that his men had managed to save all but one of the crew of this other wreck but unfortunately the young cabin boy drowned. The *Little Test* was carrying a cargo of copper ore, far less pilferable, but nevertheless the Collector still had to provide guards to ensure that the vessel itself was not plundered.

The Customs were not very lucky in their search for the plundered cargo but one farmer and his labourer had their cart searched by Coastguards and one hundredweight of tobacco was found hidden under sacking. At the court hearing several witnesses came forward to swear that there was no tobacco in the cart until deliberately placed there by the revenue men, but the local magistrate refused to accept their evidence and both men were given the maximum penalty – £100 fine.

There is no other record in the Customs papers of any other persons being convicted of 'stealing or harbouring wrecked goods', nor indeed did there seem to be any Customs sales of wrecked goods from the vessel, so it must be assumed that most of the cargo of the *John Lilley* did indeed go 'to feed the hungry and clothe the poor'.

Robinson Crusoes
and Old Salts

Although the most dramatic rescues and tragic shipwrecks in the Bristol Channel relate to large, or relatively large, sailing or steam ships, over the years the Channel has been the scene of numerous shipping accidents to small vessels and yachts. This has been especially so as the volume of commercial traffic has decreased and the activities of leisure sailors have greatly increased. Both the following accidents made the headlines and both occurred before the days of the fast inshore lifeboats, but they clearly illustrate that at certain times and in certain weather conditions the Bristol Channel can be a most dangerous waterway whatever the size of the vessel.

One story started as a pleasant weekend trip across the Channel from Penarth to Weston-super-Mare. The year was 1934 and the month was July. What indeed could be better than a gentle sail across the Channel on a fine summer's weekend? Who would have thought that such a harmless pleasure trip would end in near tragedy.

William Mordey, a consultant marine engineer at Newport, owned a rather fine 42 ft ex-Naval pinnace called *Silver Star*. Mordey belonged to a well-known shipping family and was a very experienced sailor and navigator holding a captain's certificate. His nephew, Cedric Howell, also from Newport, had persuaded his uncle to take his boat across to Weston to visit his aunts. The third man of the small 'crew' was Mr Cliff Williams of Penarth, who went along 'for the ride'.

They set off from Penarth about mid-day on Saturday 14th July and the crossing was quite without incident, although by the time they arrived off the beach at Weston there was a rather stiff westerly wind blowing and the sea was getting up so much that it proved quite impossible to land. They were forced to shout through a megaphone to the ladies waiting on the sands, wave goodbye and then set a return course for Penarth as the weather seemed to be closing in rather quickly.

Mr Mordey decided to set a course west-north-west, which would take them between the two islands of Flat Holm and Steep Holm towards Barry, which provided a better haven in bad weather than Penarth. When the vessel was virtually half-way across the Channel the wind became 'terrific and the seas were very heavy'. The *Silver Star* shipped a 'green sea' over her bow and her condition began causing some concern. Very soon the sea-water got down to the magneto and the engine cut out. Whilst Mr Mordey was trying to dry out the magneto, Mr Howell said that he had the distinct impression that the pinnace was drifting rather rapidly onto the rocks on the western side of Flat Holm. The anchor was quickly dropped over the side but the chain snapped. The vessel was now drifting towards the rocks at an alarming speed so it was decided to abandon her for a small dinghy, which was being towed behind. However, before they even had a chance to get into the dinghy it turned turtle and was thrust away against the rocks.

Their only salvation now seemed to be to swim ashore – some 20 yards or so to the reef. Mr Howell has given a vivid description of their ordeal:

'... Cliff Williams dived among the rocks and I remember thinking it was the end of him but he surfaced and made land. My uncle jumped in backwards spreading his mackintosh out to catch the air pockets to stop him sinking. Then I jumped in but landed in a trough which washed me back to the boat. Fortunately the next wave washed me shorewards.

By good fortune we all made it safe and sound in time to watch the *Silver Star* breaking up. She dropped her engine and the rest of it was just an empty shell which was smashed to pieces on the rocks. We were marooned on an outer reef, standing there and mournfully watching our boat being reduced to matchwood'.

Although they had landed safely the three men were still in grave danger because of the rising tide. The island's lighthouse keeper appeared at this moment and he managed to get a line across the 20 ft gully to them and so was able to haul them across in the dinghy, which they had managed to recover. Other than their feet being badly cut by the razor-like rocks and some bruising, the men were relatively unharmed by their experience. Mr Harris, a farmer, and his wife made the party comfortable and gave them accommodation for the night.

The whole drama was being watched through the telescope on the Barry Yacht Club pavilion and the Barry lifeboat was alerted until it was seen that the skipper and crew had landed safely on the island. The lighthouse keeper, with his dressing table mirror and using the setting sun, flashed first Penarth then Barry and he received an answer from Barry. With his heliograph he sent the message 'Silver Star – total wreck – all hands safe'. Within minutes a message was telephoned to Mr Mordey's wife in Newport – 'Don't expect your husband home tonight'!

The following morning all they could salvage from the wreck was the ship's brass bell, which is still in the family's possession, and a carton of 100 rather damp cigarettes floating around; though a cut glass tumbler from the vessel was later seen gently rocking back and fro in a rock pool, completely undamaged without even a scratch on it!

Soon after, they noticed a pilot cutter come close into the shore but the crew did not see their frantic signals. It was on such an occasion that Mr Howell wished that he had become more proficient at signalling in the Scouts; as the pilot cutter turned away he said that they felt like 'three Robinson Crusoes'. Fortunately the lighthouse keeper, using two battens, once part of the Silver Star, semaphored the message 'Where are you bound?' The pilot replied on his hooter in Morse code 'I am looking for an anchorage to do a bit of fishing'. Then the keeper requested their rescue, again in semaphore. The three men owed much to the lighthouse keeper. A lighthouse had first been erected on the island in 1733 and the last keeper left in 1969 when the beacon was electrified.

The three men scrambled into the salvaged dinghy and with the use of laths from their wrecked boat, paddled over to the Cardiff pilot cutter to a warm welcome and a Sunday lunch of roast beef and Yorkshire pudding! They arrived back in Cardiff safe and sound just over 24 hours after they had sailed from Penarth.

Five years earlier, in 1929, a small railway boat left the hoists at Newport with a cargo of coal for Wick St Lawrence on the Somerset coast. Anyone watching it pass down the river Usk would not have given it a second look, so familiar were such vessels. Her name was the *Lily* and she was one of the last railway boats to ply the Bristol Channel. These were usually Severn trows, those ubiquitous working boats which were unique to the Bristol Channel and the river Severn. They were effectively a double-ended open decked barge with a very shallow draft ideally suited to the mud flats and river estuaries of the upper reaches of the Channel. The 'railway boats' gained their name from their trade of supplying coal from the Welsh ports to the Weston-Clevedon-Portishead Light Railway Company, which was a delightful, if a trifle eccentric, little line that operated from 1907 to 1940. The small village and tiny port of Wick St Lawrence situated on the river Yeo had a small coal quay used by the railway company, to where the *Lily* was bound.

The *Lily* was a rather ancient 33 ton trow equipped with an auxiliary motor, which had been crossing the Channel for the best part of 40 years. She set out on 25th January 1929 with approximately 30 tons of coal and with a crew of just two – Tom Berridge, the skipper and his mate, Jack Hunter. They had no reason to think that this trip would be any different to the hundreds of similar journeys they had made.

They had barely left the mouth of the Usk before they discovered that the vessel had sprung a leak. The tell-tale appearance of oily black water on the floor of the for'ard locker caused them some dismay, especially as the state of the tide prevented them from returning to Newport. There was no alternative but to man the pumps and hope that they managed to make the Somerset shore.

Unfortunately for them the leak proved to be more serious than they first thought and the vessel began shipping so much water that they were having great difficulty in coping with the pumping. Soon the amount of water taken on board affected the steering and the helm would not respond despite the fairly calm sea, which was quite unusual for late January. It must have been a sad realisation for the two men that they and their vessel were now completely at the mercy of the Channel's currents and tides. However hard they pumped they were only just keeping the *Lily* afloat and she was being carried along like a piece of driftwood. They passed Flat Holm and its rocky shore (very close to where the *Silver Star* came to grief) with the ebbing tide dragging the vessel down channel towards Barry Roads.

When she finally arrived in Barry Roads the tide was turning and, like a piece of flotsam, the *Lily* began to be drawn back in the direction of the Usk. They had been at the mercy of the Channel waters for over 14 hours and had been manning the pumps, without a break, for all that time. It now looked as if they would arrive back at their starting point, that is if they managed to keep the *Lily* afloat.

They decided to drop anchor and just concentrate on pumping in the reasonable hope that some vessel making for Newport on the tide would see them. Jack Hunter later said that it seemed as if they had been pumping for days. It was back breaking work and this prolonged exertion finally took its toll of the old skipper – he was close on 68 years old – and he collapsed. As Jack Hunter revived him the boat was sinking lower and lower in the water. Then, as if by an act of providence, a pilot cutter from Newport, the *Nancy*, which was returning to port on the flowing tide, saw the sinking vessel and came alongside to give them a tow. As the tow was taken up the sudden strain proved to be too much for the old *Lily* and her timbers began to fall apart. Both men swam for the 'Nancy' as their ship sank.

Once the *Nancy* had landed the two intrepid sailors at Newport, the news of their long ordeal and their rescue quickly went round the port. A newspaper report suggested the courage and determination of these 'two old salts' exemplified why 'British seamen had conquered the Seven Seas'! The two sailors returned to their Somerset homes, rather appropriately, by rail. Jack Hunter's final comment on their adversity was 'I don't want another 20 hours like that one, I can tell you'. Almost word for word what William Mordey was to express five years later. At least, unlike many shipwrecks in the Bristol Channel, all five men survived to tell their tales.

The Sands of Silk

Today the Cefn Sidan Sands have lost much of their notoriety. They form a splendid five mile long stretch of beach along the Dyfed coast between the Loughor estuary and the entrance to the Gwendreath river, fronting Carmarthen Bay. These firm sands with their backing dunes are a most popular attraction for summer visitors. However, not too many years ago, the very name of Cefn Sidan struck terror into the hearts of many a sailing master, especially those who regularly traded to the nearby ports of Carmarthen, Pembrey, Burry and Llanelli.

For centuries the Sands had been rightly feared as one of the most dangerous and treacherous areas in the whole of the Bristol Channel and they had become the final resting place of many a fine sailing vessel. Their name, which can be freely translated as 'silky water' or 'sands of silk', greatly belies their dangers – vicious strong currents combined with a prevailing on-shore wind make them most menacing to shipping. The Sands could be dry as much as nine ft in places and the Admiralty's 'Sailing Directions' gave a grave warning to masters: '. . . [they] are liable to shift during westerly gales; the bar should never be taken except with local knowledge . . . Owing to the shallowness of the water fronting the bar, and to the great swell generally rolling up from the south-west, the locality is subject to blind rollers, very dangerous to boats. Even in fine weather an outside ground swell produces a dangerous sea, the tide also runs very strong'. Allied to these natural dangers were the brutal wrecking proclivities of the local people, which indeed made a daunting mixture of danger and menace – enough to frighten even the most doughty sea captain.

During the early years of the 19th century there were many wrecks on the Cefn Sidan Sands. In October 1810 the *Union*, sadly off-course on a voyage from London to Cadiz, came to grief with the loss of all hands, and on the very same day another vessel was stranded on Pembrey Sands. A particularly bad storm two days before Christmas 1816 resulted in no less than four ships wrecked on the Sands with a heavy loss of life. But of all the unfortunate vessels that have foundered on the Sands perhaps the most famous, or infamous, was the *La Jeune Emma* on 21st November 1828.

As the name suggests, she was French and came from Cherbourg. On what proved to be her last voyage, she was bound for Le Havre from Martinique in the West Indies with a cargo of rum, sugar, spices, coffee, cotton and ginger. For the vessel to be in Carmarthen Bay at all suggests a gross error of navigation. It was thought that the master, Captain De Chatellan, had mistaken Land's End for Finisterre and that the light from the Lundy Island lighthouse was wrongly identified as the Ushant light. The captain was sure that he was sailing northwards to make a landfall at the Lizard, blissfully unaware of the perilous and fateful course he was taking, though in mitigation it must be said that there was a dense fog all along the Bristol Channel and in those days there were far fewer lights to guide mariners. The *La Jeune Emma* finally grounded on the eastern tip of the Cefn Sidan Sands.

The *Cambrian Weekly* reported the tragic wreck:

'When she struck ... a scene of consternation and horror ensued which baffles description. The whole of the crew and passengers rushed on deck, over which the sea broke dreadfully and before daylight 13 souls had been swept away by the breakers and had met a watery grave ... Colonel Coquelin of the French Marine and his daughter, an interesting young lady, niece to Josephine, Empress of France and consort of Bonaparte [Napoleon had died seven years earlier] and their two servants, who all perished, six only were saved. The assistance rendered to the few unfortunate [surely fortunate?] survivors needs no eulogism of ours ...'

Of the 13 that lost their lives, nine were given a Christian burial at the Norman church at Pembrey on 28th November and in the burial register the young lady's age is given as twelve years. She was interred in the same grave as her father in order, according to the vicar, 'so there to unite with its kindred clay'. Another contemporary report states that 14 young ladies of Pembrey 'attired in deep mourning attended the remains of Mademoiselle Coquelin to the house appointed for all the living'. This sombre and sad ceremony was in stark contrast to what had happened elsewhere.

Though the loss of the vessel and the 13 lives was lamentable, the days following the shipwreck proved to be even more appalling. Before the burial the looters were busy plundering the wreck and its cargo. The crew's belongings and prized possessions were not sacrosanct, they were stolen without either compunction or compassion. One local man is said to have found a cask of rum on the shore and using a purloined snuff

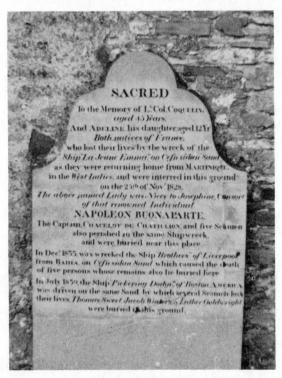

The headstone in Pembrey churchyard where Colonel Cocquelin of the French Marine and his daughter, niece of Empress Josephine of France, were interred together in 1828. (Picture: David Prosser)

box as a cup, he proceeded to drink himself into a stupor and then later proudly boasted of the fact! The plundering was so bad that the local militia from Carmarthen were ordered to the scene with loaded muskets ready for the worst, but by the time they had arrived the locals had virtually picked the vessel clean and most of the cargo had disappeared. The *Carmarthen Journal* severely censured the local people; 'the conduct of certain wretches, who are a disgrace to their species, and who without that absolute want of feeling and pity, which marks the extreme of human depravity ... monsters who, instead of succouring, robbed and ill-treated the helpless and the perishing...'

The sad story now took on a rather macabre twist. When another body from the wreck was recovered just a few days after the burial, it was interred in the same grave as his shipmates. When the grave was reopened, one of the coffins had been disturbed, the body was missing and all that remained was a sailor's blue shirt. It was said that this desecration caused 'a great sensation' and lurid tales of resurrection men abounded locally.

At the end of the year even further controversy broke out over the wreck when one of the few lucky survivors wrote from France to maintain that at the very moment when *La Jeune Emma* struck the Sands, a vessel passed so close as to be within hailing distance but for some reason the captain chose to ignore the cries for help. The writer implied that the master had deliberately disregarded the distress calls in order not to jeopardise his vessel and the lives of his crew. The truth of this assertion was never resolved.

The tragic tale of this wreck continued to cause sensation long after 1828. In 1847 a book on travels around Carmarthenshire was published wherein the writer alleged that some of the crew of *La Jeune Emma* had been barbarously treated by the looters and furthermore that young Adeline Cocquelin had her fingers cut off to steal her rings. It is presumed that the writer had obtained this story from a local surviving witness, though it must be said that with such sensational shipwrecks and incidents stories tend to be exaggerated in the re-telling. Unfortunately this gruesome story gained a certain credence and was repeated for many years afterwards, adding to the already infamous reputation of the coast.

Abandon Ship

It was on the afternoon tide of 12th November 1949 that the Spanish steamship the *Monte Gurugu* slipped out of Newport docks with a full cargo of coal – some 5,000 tons – for its home port of Bilbao. The 'Monty boats' as they were familiarly called in shipping circles, were regular visitors to the South Wales ports; they normally arrived with cargoes of pit-props, often piled perilously high on the open decks, or heavily laden with iron ore. Their crews were popular with the Welsh dockers, not only for their friendly and happy dispositions but also for the cheap Spanish brandy they liked to smuggle to help bolster their very low wages. The *Monte Gurugu* was one of the oldest vessels of the large 'Monte' fleet; she had been built in 1921, was 3,554 tons and carried a crew of 37 men.

On her first evening out in the Bristol Channel the vessel ran into very heavy weather. There was a particularly strong north-westerly gale blowing and as she laboured along the coast, she was pounded by tremendous waves. Later it was stated that the seas that were running that night were the worst encountered in the Channel for many years. However, Captain Luis Numalrz was not too concerned as he was well experienced in the Bay of Biscay, which was even more notorious for its heavy seas. Of this stage of the voyage he later said, 'It was no problem though the weather she was very rough but the grand seas made our progress very slow and the engines had to work very hard.' The fact that the vessel was fully laden helped her stability; but indeed she probably bore a strong resemblance to John Masefield's 'Dirty British coaster' – 'with a salt-caked smoke stack, battling through the Channel in the mad March days'!

Early on the following afternoon (13th) the vessel had almost passed out of the Bristol Channel, approaching Hartland Point with Lundy Island on her starboard side. The conditions had not improved, in fact they had marginally worsened and the *Monte Gurugu* was now heading into the full fury of the Atlantic Ocean. She was then subjected to a particularly vicious series of waves which broke the rudder adrift and she was suddenly left rolling around helplessly in the huge seas. Within what seemed like just a few minutes, the vessel developed a leak in the forward hold and quickly began to take in water at an alarming rate, making the situation very serious. The captain later stated that it had all happened so quickly that they had barely time to hoist distress signals and transmit an SOS mess-

P.A.-Reuter photo

The Ilfracombe lifeboat brings survivors of the Spanish ship Monte Gurugu into Ilfracombe on Sunday. The ship blew up off Lundy Island on her way from Newport to Genoa. See news story.

Search Goes On For Men Missing From Blown-up Steamer

The Ilfracombe Lifeboat pictured bringing in survivors from the *Monte Gurugu* in November 1949. (Picture: South Wales Argus Ltd.)

age. However, the radio operator just managed to send a desperate signal – 'Send help quickly. Now abandon ship.'

Less than half an hour after transmitting this urgent appeal for help, the two ship's lifeboats were launched but unfortunately one was severely damaged against the side of the sinking ship and the twelve crewmen flung into the sea. The radio operator and another member of the crew managed to get away in the ship's dinghy. The captain was the last man to leave the vessel and he had no alternative but to dive into the sea, where he was fortunately dragged into the one surviving lifeboat. Within a quarter of an hour of the ship being abandoned, one of the boilers burst with a great explosion and the *Monte Gurugu* broke into two parts and rapidly disappeared beneath the waves. She sank a couple of miles off Bull Point.

The captain later described the dramatic scene to a local reporter:

> 'The terrific force of the seas smashed in the bow plates, and the ship began to take in water. When it started to settle by the bows, I tried to turn with the idea of racing for the shore but found that the rudder had been broken. She was rapidly sinking, and I gave orders to abandon ship. The water got into her boilers and as we got about 100 yards from the ship there was a terrible explosion as the boilers burst. Whatever we seemed to do we couldn't stop our boat being driven to the shore.'

The distress signal had been picked up by a tanker, the *Lady Frederica*, which was about 25 miles away and its captain immediately altered course to see whether they could offer any assistance. But within a short steaming time the captain radioed that his vessel was making very heavy weather and 'he wished not to proceed or will smash ourselves up.' The message had also been picked up on shore by the Coastguard and the three nearest lifeboat stations were alerted – Appledore, Clovelly and Ilfracombe.

The Clovelly lifeboat, *William Cantrell Ashley*, was a brand new motor boat of the latest 'Liverpool' class and had only been on station for a matter of months. When the message came into the station it was low tide and the lifeboat took nearly two hours to negotiate a gap in the rocks, as their normal passage had been blocked by fallen rocks due to the storm. They searched for survivors around Hartland Point and they were later informed that the vessel had sunk further away across the other side of the bay.

The *Violet Armstrong*, the Appledore lifeboat, had better luck with their launch and was soon out in the bay also looking for survivors. The crew thought that the distressed vessel was on fire but what they had actually seen were the boilers bursting. The damaged but empty ship's lifeboat was found first and soon after five bodies were recovered from the sea. Just a few minutes later the lifeboat crew picked up one crew member, who was barely alive and needed urgent medical attention so they swiftly made tracks for the nearest port – Ilfracombe

When the message was received at Ilfracombe, the conditions for launching could not have been worse. It was reported that 'the seas were breaking right over the pier'. But, quite undaunted by the formidable seas that were running, the coxswain, Cecil Irwin, successfully got away in the *Richard Silver Oliver*, another 'Liverpool' class lifeboat. He had decided to make for Woolacombe Bay and run in close to the shore in the hope that they could intercept any boats that were driven that way by the prevailing wind and the tide. This hunch, based on his long experience of the waters along the coast, paid off handsomely. They sighted a boat filled to overbrimming with survivors and it was barely 30 yards or so from the breaking sea. The ship's lifeboat appeared to be in grave danger of overturning, there were only four oars and the Spanish seamen were so exhausted that they could not control the boat. Irwin brought his boat in as close as he thought prudent and attempted to get a grapnel on board. His first attempt failed but on the next run-in the grapnel held and they were able to drag the boat into deeper water to transfer the exhausted men. The lifeboat managed to get all the 23 survivors on board and sped back to Ilfracombe as fast as the conditions would allow. Once the bedraggled but thankful crewmen were landed and quickly bundled off to hospital, the lifeboat put out to sea again to search the area. Meanwhile the ship's dinghy had been thrown up on Woolacombe Sands. The wireless operator had survived the ordeal but the other seaman was dead.

Despite a long and tiring search no other survivors were

found by the Ilfracombe lifeboat. The following day (14th) the search was continued by the lifeboats, assisted by aircraft from RAF Chivenor, but no further signs were seen of the missing six men.

The chief steward of the *Monte Gurugu*, Julio Gangoite, had managed to keep up the spirits of his shipmates by singing old Spanish songs, which reminded them of their homes. He was most eager to let his relatives know that he was safe and more especially his wife, as she was expecting a baby in about a month's time. The lucky survivors were effusive in their praise of the way they had been treated in Ilfracombe and the chief officer, Juan Bliden, summed up their thoughts and feelings – 'we all owe our lives to the bravery of the crew of the lifeboat'.

This debt of gratitude was fully recognised by the Spanish Government. The Spanish Lifeboat Society awarded its silver prize medal to each coxswain of the three lifeboats involved in the rescue and there were diplomas for each crew member. These well deserved awards were presented in an official cere- mony held on Ilfracombe pier on 30th June 1950. The two coxswains from the Appledore and Ilfracombe lifeboats also received medals from the Royal National Lifeboat Institution – a bronze and silver respectively. The last words on this sad incident are best left to the Spanish captain of the *Monte Gurugu*; 'I will never, ever forget the sight of the lifeboat coming towards us. God had answered our prayers'.

The Incredible Journey

There have been many memorable and gallant rescues by the lifeboats stationed along the Bristol Channel. However, probably the most outstanding and spectacular rescue took place in January 1899 on the north Devon coast. It has rightly achieved immortal fame in the history of the Royal National Lifeboat Institution.

On 12th January there was a full north-westerly gale blowing directly onto the shore; some contemporary reports suggest that it was of 'hurricane force', though in those days the term was rather imprecisely used. Nevertheless there was no doubt that it was a most severe gale – heavy seas pounded the coast from Hartland Point to the Avon estuary. It was seven o'clock in the evening when a telegram from the owner of the Anchor Hotel at Porlock was delivered to the Rev Hockley, the secretary of the Lynmouth lifeboat. It stated that there was a large sailing vessel out in the bay that seemed to be in great difficulties, it was drifting ashore and sending up signals for assistance. The tide at Lynmouth had passed high water and the sea was so rough that it proved quite impossible to launch the lifeboat from there. The gale had brought down the telegraph lines so no nearby lifeboat stations could be alerted.

The coxswain, Jack Crocombe, and his crew discussed the situation and they came to only one conclusion – the lifeboat would have to be launched from Porlock. In those days lifeboats were often hauled some distance before being launched but the Lynmouth decision almost beggars description for its sheer spirit and audacity. The distance between the two places is almost twelve miles, which would present a formidable and arduous task in any circumstances. However, the journey to Porlock would result in a long and steep climb out of Lyn-

Gold, Silver and Bronze Medals with Vellum Thanks of the R.N.L.I. (Picture: Royal National Lifeboat Institution)

mouth, then a long pull along one of the most exposed parts of the coast, which in places is at least 1,000 ft above sea level, before descending a one in four gradient hill into Porlock to reach sea level once again! The lifeboat weighed close on to three and a half tons and would have to be hauled by horse and man power with oil lamps as the only illumination and all this endeavour would be undertaken in really atrocious conditions – a howling gale with driving torrential rain. Even with today's modern equipment it would be a difficult task, as anyone who has driven the same route today would readily agree. Ninety or so years ago it showed such utter determination and resolution by the crew and their helpers that one is amazed at such dedication to their lifeboat service – it really was a most incredible journey.

Sixteen horses were provided to pull the lifeboat carriage and an advance party of men were sent ahead with a horse and cart to dig out the roadside banks to widen the road sufficient to take the carriage. The epic journey started at about eight o'clock in the evening and most of the villagers turned out to help get the carriage up the steep hill. Arriving at the top the first setback was encountered, one of the wheels of the carriage came adrift and it took considerable effort to replace it. By now everybody was thoroughly soaked to the skin, the rain was unrelenting, and many of the helpers decided to turn back and return home, just leaving a party of about 20 men (mostly the crew) to continue the journey.

Along the top of the cliffs near Glenthorne they met their second obstacle – a stone wall – and they were forced to remove a length of it to allow free passage for the lifeboat. When they arrived at County Gates, a serious problem arose because the carriage would not pass along the narrow lane. It was then decided to take the lifeboat off the carriage and place it on skids, which made it possible to move it forward manually at about six ft at a time. The men worked in pairs and the lane was so narrow that there was barely room for them to squeeze between the wall and the lifeboat; it was particularly slow and back-breaking work, which must have greatly sapped their energy. Meanwhile the carriage had been taken across several fields to join the road a mile or so further on where the path was wider. The sheer effort required to get the lifeboat back onto the carriage was formidable and the following descent down the hill into Porlock tested their strength and will-power to the full. All the men were needed just to hold the lifeboat and carriage back to prevent it crashing into the horses. Even when they finally reached the village of Porlock their troubles were still not over. In one of the narrow lanes they had to remove some stones from the corner of a cottage in order to manoeuvre the lifeboat around a tight bend. It is said that the occupant – an old lady – was none too pleased, though her attitude changed when she realised that the lifeboat was going to a vessel in distress!

The crew were greeted with the news that the sea wall at Porlock had been washed away and that the main road was impassable, so they were forced to take a higher road to gain access to the beach. Along this road they encountered a large tree blocking the way, which was unceremoniously sawn down and manhandled out of the way. The men and their lifeboat finally reached the beach at about six o'clock in the morning, the quite incredible journey had taken nearly ten hours. The crew refused all offers of food and refreshment and set about launching their boat although it was still blowing very hard and there was a heavy sea running with large breakers.

The eight-oar lifeboat, once successfully afloat, was rowed

into the teeth of the gale and it took close on to one and a half hours to reach the stricken ship. She turned out to be the *Forrest Hall*, a large barque of 1,900 tons from Liverpool with a crew of 15. The vessel was in ballast from Belfast bound for her home port. She had been under tow but the ropes had parted and shortly after the rudder had been carried away in the storm. The master, Captain James Aliss, realised that the only hope of saving his vessel would be to ride out the storm, providing the anchors held. Somewhat as a precaution he hoisted distress signals, which resulted in the lifeboat's astounding journey.

When the Lynmouth lifeboat arrived on the scene, the coxswain advised the captain that it would be best to wait for daylight when it was hoped that a fresh towline could be got on board. Just after dawnbreak the tug *John Jolliffe* from Liverpool appeared and the lifeboat crew managed to get a rope from the tug onto the *Forrest Hall*. Some of the lifeboatmen boarded the vessel to help get the anchors up, though in truth they were far more exhausted than most of the ship's crew.

The tug now made for Barry Docks with the stricken vessel in tow and despite much persuasion to the contrary, the lifeboat crew were determined to accompany them across the Channel in case they might be needed. As the *Forrest Hall* had no steerage, she began drifting towards the dangerous Nash Sands. The captain signalled for the help of another tug and fortunately there was another Liverpool tug, the *Sarah Jolliffe*, nearby, which answered the call. The two tugs brought the stricken vessel and the lifeboat safely into Barry Docks. They arrived at six o'clock in the evening of 13th January. The lifeboatmen were thoroughly exhausted; they had not slept or eaten for over 24 hours. At Barry they were royally received at a local hotel and tended by the Shipwrecked Mariners Society. The following day the lifeboat set off back across the Channel, having a tow for much of the way. Needless to say it returned to Lynmouth in triumph.

The lifeboat that took part in this epic service was the *Louisa*, which had been on station since 1887 and was replaced only seven years after her hour of glory. There had been a lifeboat at Lynmouth since 1869 and the station remained until 1944 when the last lifeboat was removed. During its 75 years the various crews saved 71 lives.

Women and Children First

The majority of the most famous shipwrecks are those relating to passenger or emigrant vessels, when the scale of the human tragedy is remembered for decades; the *Royal Charter* off the coast of Anglesey in 1859 and the *Deutchsland* off the Essex coast in 1875 are just two such examples of many. Indeed, in just six years between 1847 and 1853 there were no less than 59 emigrant ships lost on the way to America with a frightful cost in human lives.

The Bristol Channel did not have a large passenger or emigrant port, at least not to compare with Liverpool, London or Glasgow. Bristol did have a relatively small passenger and emigrant trade to the Americas, more especially the West Indies, and the South Wales ports had a very small share of the emigrant traffic to America and Australia. But what the Bristol Channel did have in great profusion was ferry and packet traffic both with Ireland and across the Channel. Before the days of the Severn railway tunnel there were literally hundreds of small packet and ferry vessels plying to and fro, up and down, and across the Channel with passengers and goods. With this proliferation of small 'passenger' vessels dashing about the Channel, just on the law of averages some were bound to come to grief.

The *William and Mary* was a small sailing packet of just over 300 tons, which sailed weekly from Bristol to Waterford in southern Ireland. She normally left Bristol on a Friday (depending on tides) and returned the following Thursday. In 1817 she had been on the regular service for three years. The vessel left Bristol, called at Pill, a small port on the Avon, to pick up mails before sailing non-stop to Waterford. On 28th October 1817 at about nine o'clock in the evening, all seemed set fair. By all

A 19th century engraving of the Nash Point lighthouses, erected in 1832 to mark the tortuously narrow channel between the sands and the mainland.

accounts the evening was clear and there was nothing more than a moderate breeze. Suddenly she struck a reef of rocks, known as the Wolves, just a mile or so west of Flat Holm. It is not clear whether the vessel carried any lifeboats; this was many years before such provisions were required by law. She was said to have sunk 'within minutes' of striking the rocks. There were 55 passengers on board including 22 women and children, and only one person survived, clinging to the topmast which remained above the waves. Fifty bodies were ultimately recovered and they were all buried in a large communal grave on the island, which was marked with a large single gravestone. This stone has sadly disappeared, said to have been built into the wall of the island's hospital (the cholera hospital built in 1883).

A few years later a public outcry followed one of the worst shipping disasters ever in the Bristol Channel. Within twelve months of the tragedy lighthouses were erected on the mainland to warn mariners of the dangers of the Nash Sands.

The small schooner-rigged paddle steamer the *Frolic* had started a regular packet service from Haverfordwest to Bristol, calling at Carmarthen and Tenby, in 1830. The *Frolic*, part-owned by the Bristol General Navigation Company, was a neat and trim little vessel, which had been built in Scotland in 1827. The new packet service provided a useful link with Bristol and West Wales, which also connected with the considerable Irish traffic into and from Milford Haven.

On the night of 16th March 1831 the vessel was on the last leg of her trip to Bristol. Sailing conditions were reasonably good, a fresh breeze from the south-west kept the Channel free of fog but it was cloudy and overcast with no moon. At about three o'clock in the morning she was off the south Glamorgan coast, when suddenly she struck the Nash Sands, a six mile stretch of sandbanks running north-west from Nash Point. It was reported that the vessel 'immediately went to pieces and every soul perished'. There were nearly 80 passengers on board including several high ranking military officers and many women and children. Many bodies were recovered on the shore over the following days. Perhaps the saddest were those of a mother and her baby, who were found 'fast locked in each other's arms'.

The sad disaster caused a terrific furore, not only locally but nationally. The Elder Brethren of the Trinity House were forced to take swift action and in 1832 two lighthouses were built 300 yards apart at Nash Point. Their lights marked the narrow but safe channel known as the 'inner passage' between the Sands and the mainland. This stretch of coast, once so dangerous to shipping, now forms part of the Welsh Heritage Coast. In 1840 the Lords of the Admiralty on their annual inspection in a Naval vessel, the *Black Eagle*, became stranded on Nash Sands and but for the fact that the sea was calm and the vessel managed to get free on the next tide there could have been another disaster. Perhaps their mishap had a bearing on the Admiralty sailing instructions of 1868, which warned 'No vessels ought to approach any part of the Sands except with a smooth sea'!

One of the features of the Bristol Channel was the number of passenger pleasure steamers that plied their trade between the South Wales ports and the seaside resorts of the Somerset and north Devon coasts. From the late 1880s these pleasure steamers, especially the Campbell white funnel fleet, became familiar sights in the Channel during the summer season. Their safety record was quite amazing. During their heyday millions of passengers were carried and yet there were no serious accidents ... but there were several remarkable escapes!

In July 1926 the *Cambria*, a paddle steamer, went aground at Hele Bay near Ilfracombe in dense fog. Luckily enough the sea was quite calm and the Ilfracombe lifeboat, the *Richard Crowley*, managed to get all the 500 passengers off without a single mishap, though it took a fair number of journeys to achieve! The vessel was refloated on the next tide.

One of the most remarkable escapes happened in fairly recent times. The motor vessel *Prince Ivanhoe*, one of the last pleasure vessels in the Bristol Channel, was operating on an excursion trip from Penarth to Minehead then diagonally across the Channel to Mumbles, from whence it cruised along the Gower Coast. The day was 3rd August 1981 and according to the local newspaper 'the four hundred and fifty passengers were enjoying the calm sea and the beautiful summer weather.'

It was mid-afternoon as the *Prince Ivanhoe* was gently sailing along the Gower Coast, only about a quarter of a mile from the shore 'to give the passengers a good view of the coast'. The vessel passed Oxwich Point and turned into Port Eynon Bay before heading back to Mumbles. She was just coming out of the bay when there was a very loud rumbling noise followed by a sharp bang and almost simultaneously the engines stopped. It was quickly obvious to the captain, David Neill, that the vessel had been holed, as she started taking in water, but at this stage he did not have any idea just how serious was the damage.

He decided to make an announcement to the passengers that the vessel had struck an underwater obstacle and although there was no grave danger, as a precaution passengers should put on lifebelts and go the muster stations. It was reported that although there was some understandable alarm amongst the passengers, there was no sign of panic and that both the passengers and crew appeared remarkably calm.

Meanwhile the captain had already transmitted an SOS call, which was picked up by the Coastguard station at Mumbles, who immediately alerted the RAF air-sea rescue helicopters and

The pleasure steamer *Cambria* aground at Hele Bay near Ilfracombe in July 1926. (Picture: Ilfracombe Museum)

the Horton inshore lifeboat station, as well as the Mumbles lifeboat. Since the vessel was taking in a considerable amount of water, indeed it was later stated that if she had been in deeper water she would have sunk in about 40 minutes, the captain considered his only course of action was to try and beach her as soon as possible. Fortunately the engines restarted and the vessel was brought inshore very gingerly until she came to rest on the sand just about 100 yards from the shore and right in the centre of the bay.

One further complication was that the tide was on the make and it was thought that within four to five hours the *Prince Ivanhoe* was likely to be completely submerged. It was therefore essential to remove the passengers off the vessel as swiftly as possible. The Horton and Port Eynon inshore lifeboats, which were the first on the scene, completed an endless number of trips carrying the passengers to the safety of the beach. The passengers, it was said, queued patiently for their turn, though in the time-honoured tradition of the sea women and children were

All the rescue services at hand in the rescue from *Prince Ivanhoe* beached in Port Eynon Bay, August 1981. (Picture: South Wales Evening Post)

landed first. The whole operation took over an hour and it went most smoothly. By the time the last passenger was taken off, the water had risen to the level of the promenade deck. When the Mumbles lifeboat *Pentland* arrived they took off the navigational instruments, ship's stores and finally the crew. It proved to be a perfectly executed rescue operation and the passengers were full of praise for the ship's crew and the lifeboatmen. One elderly passenger suffered a heart attack and later died in hospital but otherwise there were no casualties. Letters of appreciation from the Royal National Lifeboat Institution were sent to the coxswains of both the Mumbles and Horton lifeboats.

The enquiry was undetermined just what wreck remains the *Prince Ivanhoe* had struck. It was certainly near to where a large steamship the *Eldon Park* had foundered in 1940 but also, just two weeks earlier, a fishing vessel the *Orian* had sunk quite close by. Nevertheless it was quite clear to all, that the captain's quick and positive action had averted what could have been a major disaster.

The Trinity House, along with a salvage tug, attempted to blow up the remains of the *Prince Ivanhoe* into small parts but the operation was not too successful and it was not until August 1984 – three years after the accident – that the last pieces of the *Prince Ivanhoe* were brought ashore.

Wreckers and Wrecking

There has been considerable nonsense written about wrecking and wreckers. As a county Cornwall has appeared to have cornered the market in this brutal activity if one is to believe the numerous tales of vessels being deliberately lured onto the shore by flashing lights. Some of the gruesome stories of wreck survivors being brutally murdered owe more to the vivid imaginations of writers throughout the years, than to documented and well-researched evidence. Nevertheless tales of wrecking are deeply embedded in the folk-lore of the Bristol Channel coasts – especially along north Devon, Cefn Sidan, the Gower and Glamorgan. On close inspection most of these legends relate to the looting of wrecked vessels of their equipment, cargoes and the crews' possessions, rather than to premeditated acts of wrecking. Certainly there is undeniable evidence to prove that the plundering of vessels did go on to a considerable extent along most of the Bristol Channel shores, particularly in the 18th and early 19th centuries.

The deliberate and inhuman murder of wreck survivors would have largely gone unrecorded and there are no references in any official papers that even hint at such crimes being committed, much of the so called 'evidence' being mainly based on myths and superstitions handed down from generation to generation. For instance there is a Welsh superstition that any man helped from the sea after a wreck was stolen from the sea itself, and that a life stolen from the sea brought no luck either to the survivor or his saviour. It was thought that the sea would in the end retrieve its loss, sometimes by taking both lives in return. In maritime law, any vessel which is driven ashore is not considered a wreck should any man or even a domestic animal escape death in her and be still alive *on board* when she strands;

Wrecking, the subject of this fine painting by Morland, was both widely condemned and widely practised. (Picture: Museum of Fine Arts, Boston, USA.)

where this occurs, the cargo is restored to the owners. Certainly in the 18th century there was a prevalent belief that if nobody survived a wreck, whether they be on board or on the shore, then the cargo was no longer anybody's property and therefore available for the plundering – hence the stories of wreck survivors being savagely beaten to death on the shores. Though such superstitions and mistaken beliefs were powerful incentives to desperate men it is very doubtful whether there were many instances of outright and wilful murder; like many smuggling tales such stories were very far removed from the truth.

Nevertheless for centuries wrecked vessels were considered to be 'God given' and the goods they provided as a precious bounty to alleviate the harsh and meagre existence of the dwellers along the coast. Indeed in north Devon they talked of 'a good wreck season as they would do of a good mackerel season, and thank Providence for both.' Certainly there is a long tradition of plundering wrecks in the Bristol Channel. In 1358 when *La Julienne*, laden with wine from Gascony, was wrecked near Portishead, the wine 'was carried away by divers men'. Just 50 years later the merchants of Barnstaple and Bideford appealed to the King to 'prevent the depredations of their stranded goods washed up on the coasts.' During Tudor times there were frequent references to 'vessels being pillaged by base people', the Gower and south Glamorgan coasts appearing to create particular problems. In 1581, the Lord President of the Marches, Oliver St John, complained about the number of Bristol vessels robbed on the Gower and also that many were 'plundered within the lymittes of Barry and Po'kerry.'

During the 18th century there were far more incidents recorded, not necessarily because wrecking became more prevalent but because the Customs service had become better organised. As it was their responsibility to ensure the security of wrecked vessels and their cargoes as 'Receivers of Wrecks', thus many more incidents were reported. The Customs records of the various Bristol Channel ports give ample evidence of the wrecking habits of 'the country people' – strangely they were always called such in official and newspaper reports.

For instance in 1737 the *Pye*, a snow (three-masted vessel) bound for Bristol with tobacco, sugar and cotton, was wrecked off Nash Point and the Customs Collector of Cardiff reported:

'. . . in next to no time there were 300 to 400 people from all parts of the country towards the hills assembled on the beach every night to pillage the cargo. The mob were very insolent. The hogsheads were all damaged, but the people had hoisted some of the cargo up the cliffs with ropes. They even set fire to the hull to get at the old nails . . . The Swansea militia were ordered out to arrest the worst gang from a little town called Bridgend, most of them were shoemakers . . .'

However, the military were not prepared to enter Bridgend unless each man received a £20 reward – an enormous sum in those days. The operation did not take place because it could not be decided just where the reward money would come from as there was precious little cargo saved.

Over the other side of the Channel, just one year later, the *Bedra* homeward bound from Ireland to Ilfracombe, went ashore at Saunton Sands on 13th October 1738 (a Friday no less!). Her cargo was estimated as over 1,300 pounds of soap and candles. The captain and his crew were determined that 'they had sooner the sea or the country people have it [the cargo] than the Customs' and so they came to an agreement with the locals to share the cargo. However, the captain's dealings with the wreckers backfired and he complained to the Customs Collector at Barnstaple, who gathered a party of officers to search the area. Not a single candle or one bar of soap was found, which is not really surprising as they were the type of goods that could be easily hidden. The captain had a lot of explaining to do and the case dragged on for several years before it finally petered out without any real conclusion.

The Cefn Sidan Sands, situated along the Dyfed coast, acquired a rare notoriety for the wrecking habits of the locals, who 'though they called themselves fishermen had their living by plundering wrecks ... a most determined set of villains, it matters not what comes in their way they will have it.' Such was their reputation that they became known as 'Gwyr y Bwelli Bach' or 'Men of the Little Hatchets' from the small hatchets that were the tools of their trade. These hatchets were used to cut ropes and sails, open locked doors, trunks and casks and, by repute, had other more violent uses. Though the Cefn Sidan wreckers did not have a monopoly of such brutal weapons, because on both sides of the Channel their use was well documented.

Clergy with coastal parishes were regularly exhorted by their superiors to preach a sermon at least once a quarter on 'the cruel and un-Christian-like enormity of plundering vessels.' Frequently local newspapers carried strong editorials condemning the 'wicked trade'. One editor had the temerity to suggest that 'we should send missionaries to those people who pillage wrecks instead of sending them to foreign countries' – and this was in the 1880s!

Charles Kingsley writing in 1846 of his beloved north Devon, expressed certain thoughts on wrecking:

'Wild folk are these here, gatherers of shellfish and laver and merciless to wrecked vessels, which they consider as their own immemorial usage, or rather right divine. It is significant how an agricultural people is generally cruel to wrecked seamen as a fishing one is merciful. I could tell you twenty stories of baysmen [Barnstaple] risking themselves like very heroes to save strangers lives and beating off the labouring folk who swarmed down for plunder from the inland hills.'

However, Kingsley's brother in law, the Rev John Chanter, who was vicar of Ilfracombe from 1836 to 1887, was far more forthright in his views. In a book published in 1887 he asserted:

'. . . In the old days the evil practice of wrecking was carried on to a terrible extent all along the coast. One method of enticing vessels ashore was to place lights in different parts along the cliffs. If the vessel was a foreigner or without a pilot, it would often make for the light, the crew thinking it was placed there to guide them in.
The *William Wilberforce*, which was wrecked at Lee, gives a terrible instance of the villainy of which the wreckers were capable . . . it was wilfully lured ashore by a man called Q, who had tied a lantern on to his donkey's tail to make it appear to the helmsman that he was perfectly free from the rocks with plenty of sea-room. The action of the donkey on the beach caused the lantern to move up and down, just as a shiplight would by the action of the waves, as causing the poor creatures to think that there were vessels anchored between them and the shore.'

The *William Wilberforce* was a large brig that came to grief at Lee Bay near Ilfracombe on 23rd October 1842. The crew had taken to their boat but unfortunately it capsized and not one survived, all seven men drowned. However, there were no local reports at the time of any looting, though the vessel was said to be carrying coal, and the Customs papers are silent on the matter.

Further along the coast to the west, the Rev R. S. Hawker was vicar of Morwenstow for over 40 years from 1834. His writings contain many lurid stories of wrecking along the north Cornwall coast, though he considered wreckers as 'a watcher of the sea and rocks for flotsam and jetsam and other unconsidered trifles which the waves might turn up to reward the zeal and vigilance of a patient man' – a subtle definition! Nevertheless he continually exhorted his parishioners from his pulpit to repair their wrecking ways. It is strange that it should be through the writings of two clergymen that some of the myths of wrecking were perpetuated.

It would be nice to think that we now live in more civilised and enlightened days but regrettably the wrecking instincts of many people are still very close to the surface. In October 1926 a German schooner *Elsa Kuchilke* went ashore at Westward Ho and literally hundreds of looters went to the wreck, stealing anything of value and, as the local newspaper reported '. . . they behaved in a most disgraceful manner, pillaging all they could lay their hands on even to personal photographs.' Coming to more recent times a yacht that was stranded off the Gower coast was stripped of valuable belongings during the night. And on 31st December 1982 a 960 ton Panamanian tanker, the *Johanna*, was stranded some 500 yards from Hartland Point lighthouse. However, this did not deter these 'modern day wreckers'. The national press expressed strong condemnation of their activities. It was said that 'the world and his wife descended upon the Point and parking was impossible for several miles inland.' The Coastguard were concerned about the safety of those who scrambled down the cliffs and often put themselves at great risk just in the hope of getting something for nothing.

It seems best, therefore, not to condemn too strongly the wreckers of yesteryear. At least they could claim that they were in greater need of the bounty so fortuitously supplied by the sea.

The Clovelly Roads

'A mighty singular place' is how Charles Dickens described Clovelly, that delightful village which tumbles headlong down to the sea, or 'the village in the glass case' to quote another writer. Before the days when it was discovered by the tourists of the 19th century, who came in their hordes by paddle steamer, Clovelly had long been well known as the only sheltered harbour along that part of the north Devon coast – said to be the most dangerous and inhospitable stretch in the whole of the country. The small harbour lies sheltered from the prevailing south-west gales and as the Admiralty's 'West Coast of England Pilot' warns '. . . with the wind westward of south, there is no safe anchorage between Land's End and Flat Holm in the Bristol Channel, with the exception of Lundy and Clovelly Roads . . .'

It is therefore surprising to discover that a number of vessels have gone to a watery grave just off the shore of this most picturesque harbour. One of the strangest incidents was that of the Finnish barque *Pollux* of some 4,000 tons, which had left Dublin on 9th November 1851 in ballast bound for Alexandria. No sooner was she out in the Irish Sea than she found herself in the midst of a most furious storm. As so often happened on such occasions, the ballast shifted dangerously and the vessel went over 'on her beam ends', which technically meant that she had heeled over to such an extent that the deck beams were nearly vertical and there was no righting momentum to bring the vessel back to her normal upright position.

Many a vessel has foundered under such conditions but the master felt that the *Pollux* could be righted by cutting away the main and mizzen (the third aftermast). This desperate and drastic action had the desired effect, the vessel righted herself but was now effectively out of control and drifted at the whim of the storm. The *Pollux* was driven into the approaches to the Bristol Channel and was sighted by two pilot cutters just off the north Devon coast. These admirable little boats seemed able to cope with almost any type of conditions and the Channel pilots were very experienced in such dangerous waters. They managed to come up close to the stricken vessel and offered their assistance to bring her into the safe haven of Ilfracombe. To their utter amazement the *Pollux*'s crew proceeded to abandon their vessel and left her in the charge of the pilots. Such a situation offered the chances of a rich bonus for them. If they were able to bring her into port safely they could justifiably claim a salvage reward. Such awards were based on a proportion of the value of the ship and any cargo she carried, with some consideration being given not only to the labour and danger involved in saving the vessel but also the state of the weather at the time.

The pilots did manage to get the *Pollux* safely into Clovelly Roads, which was quite a feat of seamanship, and the following morning the crew returned to their vessel, that is all except the master – Captain Lindstrom, who was reported as saying that he had pressing business elsewhere. Considering that he and his ship should have been well past Land's End en route to Egypt by now, one can only wonder what 'pressing business' kept the master from his stricken vessel! Meanwhile the pilots and some local fishermen attempted to get the *Pollux* into Bideford but for some unaccountable reason the crew steadfastly refused to offer any assistance. She became grounded twice and was refloated, and the Lloyd's agent, who was now on board and had more than a passing interest in the fate of the vessel, ordered the services of a tug. Within a short time of being taken in tow the Finnish crew cut away the towrope and the *Pollux* drifted up onto the beach at Clovelly very close to the entrance to the harbour.

The local Customs officer, who also acted as Receiver of Wrecks, now entered upon the scene; he deemed that the vessel was not 'a wreck' and gave instructions that all possible efforts be made to save her and her stores despite the crew's interference. The ballast was discharged and all the duty-free stores of spirits and tobacco were landed and placed under Customs seal. On the next full tide she was successfully refloated (yet again!) and was towed a little way off shore, anchored and left unguarded for the night. Though there was still a strong north-easterly gale blowing, she rode out the storm. However, by the following morning the lightened vessel was no match for the fury of the weather, both anchor cables parted and within a very short time the *Pollux* was driven ashore once again! The weather did its job properly this time, as she was smashed to pieces. What was finally left was sold a few weeks later. The extraordinary behaviour of the master and the crew was never explained, or if it was the details have not survived. The Customs report recites the bare facts and the details of the sale, which amounted to less than £50. Most of the ship's timbers were sold for firewood and, of course, the pilots did not receive any recompense for all their splendid effort.

Just 15 years later there was another wreck at almost the very same spot. A wooden paddle steamer, the *Queen*, had left Bristol with over 40 passengers and some 100 tons of cargo on board. This small paddle steamer was very well known along the north Devon coast, having served on the Hayle to Bristol packet service for the previous 14 years. Although the distance between the two ports was 150 miles, it was said that the *Queen* could make the single journey on a tide. She had completed well over 600 trips without a single incident or even a close shave. During most of these journeys the vessel had been commanded by Captain John Spray but in the previous October he had handed over his command to his son Granville, who had served his apprenticeship both as a seaman and a mate on the *Queen*.

On what turned out to be her last voyage, the *Queen* left Ilfracombe at 10.30 p.m. on 29th March 1866. The young master set the usual course, one which would have taken the *Queen* about five miles clear of Hartland Point. However, on this particular evening there was a dense fog along the coast and this may have adversely affected the navigation, because shortly before midnight the vessel suddenly and without any warning struck the Tings rocks with a terrific force. This is virtually the place where the Hartland lighthouse was built just eight years later. After considerable effort she was somehow cleared off the rocks and a return course was set for Ilfracombe. It was soon discovered that she was taking in water quite rapidly and the *Queen* was obviously badly holed. It was felt that she was unlikely to make Ilfracombe so it was decided to steam for Clovelly and try to run ashore on the beach. This operation was achieved without any further mishap and the *Queen* was beached about 50 yards from the pier of the harbour at Clovelly.

The remaining 37 passengers and most of the crew were safely ferried ashore in the middle of the night, though one can imagine what a stir this caused in the village! On the following morning the full extent of the damage was ascertained. She had been badly holed in the forrard and it was decided that all the cargo should now be landed; this operation took two days to complete. In fact it was finished just in the nick of time because soon afterwards the vessel's back broke and she became an utter wreck, quickly breaking up into pieces.

The Board of Trade enquiry into the wreck was held a few months later and the captain was found guilty of neglect in not taking a lead – measuring the depth of water near coasts. It would also appear that no proper ship's log had been kept since the son had taken over from his father. It seemed to be that the more familiar the journey became the more lax had become the captain and his crew. It was indeed fortunate that the vessel had not gone ashore along the coast from Westward Ho to Clovelly because, as 'The West of England Pilot' cautions, '. . . should the vessel have embayed the crew should stick to the ship; there is little or no chance whatever of saving life by taking to the ship's boats owing to the heavy and confused sea, which at times renders even lifeboats unmanageable'. Added to this grim warning could have been the information that the precipitous cliffs some 300 to 400 ft high, which have razor-sharp rocks at their foot, make the chances of survival very unlikely. Although these cliffs provide some of the most spectacular and awe-inspiring scenery in the whole of the country, they have caused the demise of many a vessel. A most awesome and desolate place to be wrecked upon, it could be days before wreckage was even sighted let alone before the unfortunate victims' bodies were recovered.

In February 1901 when the area was even less inhabited than it is today, the body of a seaman was found in a field near Peppercombe, some four miles east of Clovelly. This was the very first indication to the locals that a vessel had been wrecked.

When the Coastguards initiated a search of the area, wreckage was seen below a 350 ft cliff but there was no sign of survivors. It took several weeks to discover that the wrecked vessel was the *Goonlaze*, a schooner from Hayle which had left Bristol on 2nd February. Though the precise details of her last days and hours will never be known, she was believed to have tried to shelter in Barnstaple Bay but because of a sudden shift in the wind to the north-east was unable to clear the bay and was ultimately driven onto the rocks. It was also assumed that as she was so close under the cliffs, any distress rockets put up would have passed unseen. Three bodies were ultimately recovered. The poor seaman had survived the wreck and managed to scale the sheer cliff-face, only to die of his injuries and exposure when he was so near and yet so far from rescue and safety.

'At The *Pace*'

Appledore is said to be the most complete maritime community in the Bristol Channel, indeed the whole town seems to live and breathe its sea-going past and present. Its sailors have long been known as 'Bar-men' from the notorious sand bar at the mouth of the Taw and Torridge estuary. In 1815 the Customs Collector at Barnstaple reported that '... scarcely a year has elapsed without a shipwreck having taken place within the Bay [Bideford] ... some lives have been generally lost, the accident normally happening in the dark of night and two or three miles from immediate aid owing to the extent of the sands.' With so many shipwrecks along the shores it is no surprise to find that shortly after the founding of the Royal National Lifeboat Institution a lifeboat station was established at Appledore.

The aptly named *Volunteer* arrived in the port in February 1825, making it the first lifeboat to be established in the Bristol Channel. From 1852 there were no less than three lifeboats in the area – at Appledore, Northam Burrows and Braunton Burrows – all manned by seamen from Appledore. This long and very fine tradition of lifeboat service at the port has resulted in many splendid and courageous rescues with the saving of over 500 lives in the process. But however invidious it may be to select just one rescue out of so many to recognise this great tradition, the rescue of the Austrian barque *Pace* in December 1868 has justifiably passed into the maritime annals of the port. In fact the term 'at the *Pace*' became known as a mark of approbation, which firmly secured the reputations of each of the 28 participants.

During the morning of 28th December 1868 there was a very strong north-westerly gale blowing directly onshore; it was reported that 'horrendous seas were breaking over the sand-

The Lifeboat and its crew, such as the Northam Burrows' lifeboat *Hope* pictured here in the 1880s, were often at the very heart of a town or village. (Picture: North Devon Museum Trust)

banks at Bideford Bar, which was fringed with seething surf'. Just after midday a message was received from the Coastguard at Northam Burrows that two vessels had been sighted in the bay and they both appeared to be in extreme difficulties with the strong probability that they would be driven ashore.

The Austrian *Pace* was homeward bound to Fiume from Glasgow with a cargo of pig iron and had been driven wildly off course by the ferocious gale. Acting on the Coastguard's message, Joseph Cox, the coxswain of the lifeboat *Hope*, along with his son Joseph junior as second coxswain, mustered his crew and, with the *Hope* on its carriage pulled by a team of horses, followed the vessel as she struggled across the bay. By about one o'clock in the afternoon the *Pace* finally struck the sands and went aground, almost at once to be pounded by heavy seas.

With the assistance of many helpers that had followed the lifeboat, the *Hope* was finally launched to the accompaniment of rousing cheers. The 14 man crew had to use all their might and main to cope with the heavy seas, as the boat dropped into the deep troughs only to be thrust upwards onto the peaks. As one eye-witness commented, 'the boat was as upright as a ladder against a wall.'

It was a long and exhausting pull out to the stranded vessel and precise seamanship was needed to get in close enough for the bowman to throw a grapnel into the rigging. The crew of the lifeboat were being continually drenched from the waves crashing over the boat as well as cascading over the *Pace*. They shouted to the crew but there was neither sound nor sight of them. The barque appeared to be deserted. After what seemed an interminable length of time, a young lad suddenly appeared on the deck, climbed the rail and jumped directly into the lifeboat, where one of the crew managed to break his fall. Some minutes had passed without any further movement when suddenly eight men rushed to the side of the vessel and dived into the sea. The coxswain had to quickly manoeuvre his boat in an attempt to pick them up. Whilst he was using all his long experience (he had been coxswain for almost 20 years) to bring the lifeboat about in the confused seas, she went broadside on to the waves and a particularly heavy surge dashed the lifeboat against the barque. The coxswain was jammed between the vessel's overhanging stern and the lifeboat but fortunately his cork life-jacket saved him from being crushed to death. However, the violent collision had wrenched away the lifeboat's rudder.

The coxswain continued to shout at the remaining members of the crew to abandon the ship but he did not know then that the Austrian captain had ordered his crew not to throw a line to the lifeboat or indeed to abandon the vessel – it would seem that he was convinced that the *Pace* could be re-floated and saved on the next tide. Joseph Cox had little alternative in the circumstances but to cut the line and endeavour to get the rudderless lifeboat back to the shore. This he managed to accomplish with great skill and he found plenty of eager helpers to haul the lifeboat up onto the sand.

Amongst the anxious crowd on the shore was William Nicholls, an Appledore Customs officer who was also the honorary secretary of the lifeboat. Joseph Cox was eager to re-launch the lifeboat because he was certain that there were still men on the wreck. It was pointed out to him that not only had the boat lost its rudder but the crew was totally exhausted, also the seas were getting worse because of the outgoing tide. The coxswain was unconvinced by these arguments and he called for fresh volunteers. Without any hesitation enough men came forward so he, his son and another crewman, John Kelly, went out for a second rescue bid. Joseph junior steered the lifeboat with an oar.

As they closed with the *Pace* for the second time, five men could be seen in the mizzen mast (the third aftermast) but once again the heavy seas got the better of the lifeboat. Joseph junior was thrown out of the boat and without steerage the lifeboat swung broadside on to the waves and capsized, flinging all the crew into the sea. She quickly righted herself and the crew managed to scramble back on board. However, the boat now only had three oars left and with some difficulty was guided close enough to drag the coxswain aboard, injured and semi-conscious from sheer exhaustion. The journey back to the shore was fraught with danger, the lifeboat nearly capsized twice but finally she reached the beach.

By this time the crew of the Braunton lifeboat had made their way across the estuary and although they had been unable to get their boat across the stormy water at the river entrance they were quite prepared to man the *Hope* for a third rescue attempt. However, it was decided that as the tide was falling and the wrecked vessel looked in no further serious danger, a third launching was not necessary, especially as it was thought to be highly dangerous because of the state of the water.

Some hours later as the water receded, a number of Appledore men waded out to the *Pace* and helped rescue the three remaining men left clinging to the rigging – two had fallen and drowned. The captain was the last to be saved.

While this drama was unfolding, the other vessel the Coastguard had sighted in the bay was another barque, the *Leopard*, which was bound for Gloucester from the West Indies. The *Leopard* fared no better than the *Pace*, driven ashore near Westward Ho (only established and named just five years earlier). The local rocket apparatus team were quickly on the scene but had no success against the fierce gale. Then David Johns, a Coastguard boatman, volunteered to swim out to the vessel with a line. Considering the state of the sea and the fact that Johns had been a member of the *Hope* crew on the first rescue, his action was most gallant and heroic. Johns tried at least three times to board the stricken *Leopard* before he was struck on the head by some wreckage and sadly he drowned. Later another Appledore man managed to get a line aboard, which enabled all the crew to be rescued.

A fund was opened for Johns' widow and the Royal National Lifeboat Institution recognised the gallantry of the *Hope* and its crews. Joseph Cox was awarded second and third clasps to the silver medal he had received in 1801 – to merit two clasps was a unique achievement. His son, as well as John Kelly, received silver medals. Later the Emperor of Austria added his own recognition – silver crosses of merit to the two Coxs and Kelly as well as other awards to those helpers on the shore, including the Customs officer Nicholls. Twenty-eight men could later proudly declare that they had been 'at the *Pace*'.

The Women of Mumbles Head

Saturday 27th January 1883 can be recorded as a very black day for shipping on the Glamorgan and Gower coasts. Within the space of less than half a day three large sailing vessels foundered along its shores, all with a tragic and heavy loss of life.

On the previous Friday there had been a strong north-westerly gale blowing, which had caused considerable havoc to shipping in the upper reaches of the Bristol Channel; several small vessels were forced to flee for shelter and two ketches came to grief near Barry Island. By the early hours of Saturday morning the wind had backed to the south-west, worsened considerably and was now considered by the Coastguard to be of storm force. Such was the severity of the weather that most vessels had not ventured out of port and any that happened to be caught in the storm were in very grave danger of foundering or being driven ashore.

At about eight o'clock on the morning of the 27th, the German barque *Amiral Prinz Adalbert* from Danzig was battling her way along the Gower coast under storm canvas, though she had already lost most of her sails and spars. She was bound for Swansea with a full load of pitprops, which was a notoriously unstable cargo. The crew of 15 were particularly exhausted having spent the previous 36 hours or so with little respite or sleep because of their battle with the elements. The master, Captain Leibaner, signalled for a pilot to guide his vessel across Swansea Bay and into port. Considering the abysmal weather conditions it is perhaps not surprising that no pilot cutter answered the signal; it was extremely doubtful whether

A 19th century engraving of Mumbles Rocks and Lighthouse from the headland where in 1883 a crowd of spectators watched helplessly as the Ace sisters hauled the survivors of the *Wolverhampton* from the sea.

any cutter would have managed to get out of port. However, there was a tug standing close by and its master offered to guide the *Amiral Prinz Adalbert* into port. To his dismay, Captain Liebaner found that he could no longer 'wear the ship' – bring the vessel onto the other tack. He therefore had little alternative but to contract the tug *Flying Scud* to tow him into Swansea for the fee of £500, a sum he thought was grossly exorbitant.

For the first hour there were no great problems and reasonable, but very slow, progress was made. But then the barque suffered under very heavy seas, during which the tow cable parted and a second one broke soon after it was connected. The vessel's position was just under two miles from the coast, drifting rapidly closer to the shore. The port anchor failed to find bottom and although the starboard anchor held for a short time the constant pitch and roll put the single anchor under great stress. Eventually the enormous seas proved just too much and the anchor dragged, with the vessel being driven helplessly towards the shore. In less than ten minutes the barque struck the rocks just west of the Mumbles lighthouse. There was an horrendous crash and the strength of the impact brought the masts and the rigging down onto the decks. As a witness later testified, one minute it was a complete vessel and in next to no time 'her masts had been bumped right out of her. The foremast went first and, in falling, dragged down both the main and mizzen.'

Whilst the *Amiral Prinz Adalbert* was being driven to its doom, the tug had gone to alert the Mumbles lifeboat crew. The coxswain, Jenkin Jenkins, was advised most strongly not to put to sea as it could be suicidal in such adverse conditions. The Chief Coastguard officer told him, 'It's hell I tell you', to which the coxswain is reported to have replied, 'Well, hell it shall be.'

The lifeboat *Wolverhampton* had been at the Mumbles station since 1866 and its twelve man crew included no less than four of the coxswain's sons, as well as his son-in-law and a nephew. During the previous 17 years it had assisted many vessels and saved 67 lives – a fine record of service.

It took three attempts and the help of many local people to launch the lifeboat despite the fact that the slip-way was relatively sheltered. Although it was only a short distance around the headland to the wrecked vessel, the crew had to row against 'mountainous seas' and frequently disappeared from the view of the spectators on land. However, the lifeboat was finally sighted making its way through the inner passage between the lighthouse islet and the mainland, a very dangerous operation as the tide was ebbing, making the sea in the passage very turbulent. The rocks precluded the coxswain from bringing the lifeboat into the lee side of the *Amiral Prinz Adalbert*, so he therefore approached from the weather side, where the high seas made it impossible to get in any closer to throw a line aboard. Somebody on the barque threw out a lifebelt and with the aid of this a line was finally secured. The lifeboat put down her anchor and the crew started to take the first men off the vessel. The tremendous rise and fall of the waves made the operation a very hazardous business indeed.

The first two men were safely transferred to the lifeboat but just as a third man was being pulled aboard, the lifeboat's anchor parted, a heavy wave overturned the boat and dashed her against the barque. All the crew were pitched into the sea, though one man was bodily flung onto the barque. The lifeboat righted itself and the men managed to scramble on board but before they had time to regain control, she was struck by another heavy surge, which flung the boat over some half-submerged rocks. The lifeboat crew now tried to make for the shore but in the confused and angry surf four were drowned, as well as the unfortunate ship's carpenter, who had been transferred to the lifeboat. The survivors who managed to make the shore were all injured from the battering they received being dragged over the sharp rocks, several had broken limbs and all had suffered severe bruising. The coxswain had managed to swim to a small cave beneath the lighthouse though both of his legs were badly crushed. Two of the lifeboatmen were seen clinging on grimly to the lifelines on the side of the *Wolverhampton*.

It was at this time that two sisters – Jessie Ace and Mrs Margaret Evans – entered upon the scene. They had been in the lighthouse with their father, Abraham Ace, where they witnessed the dreadful wreck. They had come down to the shore to see whether they could offer assistance. Without a thought for their own safety they waded into the raging sea almost up to their shoulders and were in real danger of slipping on the

The damaged Mumbles lifeboat *Wolverhampton* recovered after the rescue attempt of January 1883. (Picture: Royal National Lifeboat Institution)

seaweed-covered rocks or being swept away by the waves that crashed about them. At first they couldn't quite reach the two lifeboatmen, but with a keen presence of mind Jessie Ace knotted their shawls together to form a makeshift lifeline and, with the help of a gunner from the fort (which was next to the lighthouse), they managed to pull the two men clear of the waves. It must be remembered that the lighthouse was on a small island cut off from the mainland so the crowd of spectators that thronged the headland were powerless to offer any assistance.

The lifeboat had been washed back into the sea off the rocks. She was still floating though quite damaged and later she was recovered. Amazingly, despite her condition and the heavy seas, the *Amiral Prinz Adalbert* did not break up and as the tide ebbed the rest of the crew were helped ashore by Abraham Ace and his two daughters; later they were transferred safely to the headland where they were taken to various houses and cottages in Mumbles, and provided with hot drinks, food and dry clothing. The barque stayed intact for another day but then slowly broke into pieces. It was said that her timbers and cargo of pitwood were strewn the length and breadth of Swansea Bay.

It was a very sad day for the small village of Mumbles. Four lifeboatmen had lost their lives and each left a widow, with a total of 19 fatherless children. The coxswain had lost two sons and a son-in-law, whose body was not recovered until about a fortnight later. Another member of the lifeboat crew – William Rogers – was missing presumed drowned, his body was never found. In such a close-knit community the whole village grieved deeply. The funeral for the lifeboatmen was attended by hundreds and there is a plaque and a memorial window in the parish church to commemorate their deaths.

The disaster evoked nationwide sympathy and a fund for the widows and orphans raised over £3,000 – a very respectable sum in those days. Jenkin Jenkins was awarded a silver medal and £50 by the Royal National Lifeboat Institution as an 'acknowledgement of his gallant conduct on the sad occasion and the severe injuries he received in the performance of his very perilous duties', though such recognition could never replace his two lost sons. Just ten years earlier he had been presented with a pair of binoculars from the German Emperor for his part in the rescue of another German vessel, *Triton*. A new lifeboat, also named the *Wolverhampton*, was supplied by that town just a fortnight later and Jenkin Jenkins, once he had recovered from his injuries, was back leading the crew on several rescue missions.

Strange to relate, the two Ace sisters did not receive any formal recognition from the Royal National Lifeboat Institution though the gunner – Hutchings – was presented with its thanks on vellum. However, the two sisters did receive all the publicity and their brave actions aroused tremendous public interest nationwide. Their photographs appeared on postcards – a sure sign of their fame – and it was claimed that Queen Victoria possessed copies. The Empress of Germany expressed her country's thanks for their valour and sent them silver brooches. But their lasting fame is enshrined in the poem *The Women of Mumbles Head*! written by Clement Scott, who was a very popular writer of the time. The poem is long and rather melodramatic in the best Victorian style:

'Bring, novelists, your note-book! bring, dramatists, your pen!
And I'll tell you a simple tale of what women do for men.
It's only a tale of a lifeboat, of the dying and the dead.
Of a terrible storm and shipwreck that happened off Mumbles
Head.
... There by the rocks on the breakers these sisters, hand in
hand,
Behold once more that desperate man who struggled to reach
the land.
'Twas only aid he wanted to help across the wave,
But what are a couple of women with only a man to save?
What are a couple of women? Well more than three craven men
Who stood by the shore with chattering teeth refusing to stir –
and then
Off went the women's shawls, sir; in a second they're torn and
rent,
Then knitting them into a rope of love, straight into the sea
they went!
... Well, many a heart beat stronger and many a tear was
shed,
And many a glass was toss'd right off to 'The Women of
Mumbles Head'.

All In A Day's Work

In any busy waterway, and the Bristol Channel is no exception, the everyday working vessels almost become part of the scenery. They are always present, always busy working and almost always taken for granted by the seamen on the more 'interesting' ships that use the Channel. Nevertheless such service vessels are essential; without the pilot cutters, the tugs, the lightships and the mud and sand dredgers, waterways and ports would come to a virtual standstill. In past years some of these vessels were more important than they are today; tugs were almost a necessity in the days of sailing ships, and before the days of modern technology the lightships of the Bristol Channel – St Gowan's, Helwick, Scarweathers, Breaksea and the English and Welsh Grounds – were reassuring and familiar sights to homecoming seamen – alas, these famous lightships have now been replaced by unmanned automatic beacons.

For several centuries the omnipresent Channel pilot cutters were perhaps the most well-known vessels operating in the Channel. These superb boats frequently ventured far beyond Lundy to pick up their contracted vessels. The pilots' knowledge and experience of the Channel waters and the seaworthiness of their cutters meant that they could sail out and survive in extreme weather and sea conditions and only a few were ever wrecked.

However, in December 1870, the small cutter *Dasher* from Cardiff came to grief on the Tusker Rock (near Porthcawl) in a very dense fog. Due to the poor visibility the cutter was not sighted for several hours. In the meantime the small vessel began to break up and with an ingenuity born out of desperation the pilot and his two assistants proceeded to build a crude raft from the wreckage. When the Porthcawl lifeboat *Good*

Deliverance arrived at the scene, the lifeboat crew found the three men vainly attempting to clear the surf in their cumbersome craft. Such fortitude and resource deserved a better reward. The three were taken on board the lifeboat leaving the remains of the cutter and their makeshift raft on the rocks.

Since 1846 a lightship had been moored about 17 miles south-west of Swansea. It marked and warned mariners of the Helwick Sands – a dangerous six mile stretch of sands to the west of Port Eynon Head. During the night of 1st September 1908 a strong westerly gale veered, backed to the north-west and greatly increased in strength. At about six o'clock in the morning the Helwick lightship was being battered by very heavy seas and one tremendous wave struck the vessel leaving in its wake considerable damage – the mast crashed down, the lifeboat was smashed and water gushed into the cabin and fo'c'sle. She began to list so badly that she was in very grave danger of foundering. Fortunately the passing *Lawrenny Castle* spotted the distress signals and when she arrived in Swansea, the captain's report was telegraphed to Tenby; it was reasoned that the Tenby lifeboat had a far better chance of reaching the lightship than the Mumbles boat considering the strength and direction of the gale.

The Tenby lifeboat *William and Mary Devey* made a very fast time to the stricken lightship – about two and a half hours – which considering it was a twelve-oar boat was a very creditable achievement, though the journey was physically demanding and exhausting. The coxswain had great difficulty in getting the lifeboat close enough to the lightship to effect a rescue. The heavy seas and the tangled mass of the mast and rigging thrashing about caused damage to the lifeboat, making the approach a most hazardous operation. With infinite patience and remarkable skill, the captain, two lamplighters and four seamen were safely transferred on board the lifeboat. The coxswain set a course for Swansea as it would have been virtually impossible to row back to Tenby in the teeth of such a ferocious gale.

The lifeboat arrived safely at Swansea with her crew on the point of exhaustion and some suffering from exposure. The crew had rowed in excess of 30 miles and had been out in the terrible weather for almost seven hours. The following day the lifeboat was towed back to Tenby – the end of an epic rescue. It was said that Captain Rees of the lightship was not too concerned about his and his crew's safety but he was deeply worried that the light had been extinguished and about the possible danger to other ships in the area. The Helwick lightship was replaced by a new vessel in 1927 and this is now safely moored in the Swansea Maritime and Industrial Museum.

In September 1953 another Tenby lifeboat *John R. Webb* went out in a force ten gale to rescue the crew of St Gowan's lightship, which was in considerable distress. The lifeboat had to make three attempts to take the crew off, such was the size of the waves which were virtually submerging the lightship. The whole rescue of the seven men took only 15 minutes and it was an operation full of courage, daring and excellent seamanship. These rescues were just two of the many that have been performed by Tenby lifeboats since the station opened in 1852.

The Bristol Channel has more dangerous sandbanks than perhaps any other waterway in the country, which are a constant hazard to shipping. The phenomenal tidal range causes the build-up of sand and mud banks, especially where it narrows; indeed it is estimated that two million tons of mud and sediment are carried past Severn Beach (the eastern limit of the Bristol Channel) on every ebb tide. The mud and sand dredgers of the Bristol Channel are vitally important in keeping the shipping channels open. These somewhat ugly and cumbersome vessels are an integral feature of the Channel waters and, considering their number and their long working hours, very few have stranded on the hazards that they are trying to clear.

Early in the morning of 18th June 1960 the *Ron Woolaway*, a sand dredger from Barnstaple, was operating just off Flat Holm. On this particular morning there was a dense fog covering the Bristol Channel, though in retrospect these weather conditions had little bearing on the subsequent accident. Suddenly, without any warning, the dredger slowly heeled over on her side and then capsized. The crew, guided by the dull and steady boom of the signal from the foghorn station, managed to swim to Flat Holm, where the seven men were well looked after by the lighthouse keeper. After an hour or so when the fog had started to clear, a sister ship *Stan Woolaway* happened to catch a glimpse of the up-turned vessel and closed in to investigate.

However, she could do little more than secure a line around the dredger to secure her and then the captain signalled for help. A tug towed the capsized boat bottom up to Penarth for examination; the dredger was new and had only been brought into service the previous week. The Barry lifeboat *Rachel and Mary Evans* took the seven men off Flat Holm. They seemed to make light of their lucky escape and their unexpected early morning swim, one commented rather laconically 'It's all in a day's work!'

By one of those strange coincidences that often happen at sea, just under seven years later (March 1967) the very same *Stan Woolaway* was returning to Barnstaple, fully laden with sand. The dredger was near Baggy Point on the north Devon coast when without any warning or apparent reason she developed a list, capsized and then sank very shortly afterwards. Fortunately all the crew were saved. For all these seamen who spend their working days out in the Bristol Channel in all kinds of weather, their unglamorous but important duties are not without a certain danger, though it may be 'all in a day's work'.

The Holiday Sea

Today it is almost impossible to imagine Barry Island as an 'island' because it is so built-up and developed as a holiday complex. Yet in the late 18th century it was an isolated and secure haunt of smugglers and even a century later Barry was still a mere hamlet of less than 50 inhabitants. The massive development of the docks changed all that and by 1900 Barry was the largest coal exporting port in the country. Barry Island soon lost its identity as an island in the early 20th century as it became the largest seaside resort in South Wales. Day-trippers in their thousands came from Cardiff and the teeming valleys beyond; they arrived by trains, brakes and charabancs attracted by the particular, if somewhat brash, charms of the resort. Indeed a day-trip to Barry Island became part and parcel of the social life of South Wales, as one Welsh poet so evocatively recalled;

> 'Let's go to Barry Island, Maggie fach,
> And give all the kids one day by the sea,
> And sherbet and bars and paper hats,
> And a rattling ride on the Figure Eight;
> We'll have tea on the sands and rides on the donkeys,
> . . . And we'll all sing together in the Cardiff train
> Down to the holiday sea.'

The 'holiday sea' was a long and fine expanse of sand which stretched along Whitemore Bay from Nell's Point in the east to Friars Point in the west – both rocky outcrops which posed a threat to the hundreds of vessels that used the port of Barry. Despite all the various amusements afforded by the resort, there was a rare and extra attraction for the countless holidaymakers thronging the beach on a summer morning in late August 1926.

The wreck of the *Valsesia*, an irresistible attraction for day trippers to Barry Island in August 1926 and for a further two months as she defeated all attempts to move her. (Picture: Brian C. Luxton)

It was the dramatic sight of a large steamer lying practically high and dry on the sands near the head of Friars Point.

The Italian steamer *Valsesia* (over 6,000 tons) was on the final leg of her long voyage from America for Barry fully laden with coal. Such an import into one of the major coal exporting ports would have been unthinkable just five months earlier but the South Wales coalfields had been on strike since 3rd May and the South Wales industries were desperate for coal. The vessel had encountered thick fog some miles off Barry Island and progressed very slowly forward continually sounding her fog-horn, but the captain was unaware that she was getting closer and closer to the Island. Almost at the last minute he realised just how near he was to Friars Point and in desperation the anchors were dropped quickly to prevent her drifting onto the rocks. The action was too late, and the weight of the fully laden vessel caused her to slip gently aground.

One of the eye-witnesses said that he could see 'the masts and the top of the funnel of the vessel above the rolling cloud of fog, the rest was a shapeless dark form.' However, as the morning sun began to disperse the fog, she could be seen quite clearly. Indeed as the news spread through the resort thousands of sightseers rushed to the scene to gaze in awe at the beached leviathan. Luckily there was no loss of life, communication was quickly established between the ship and the shore and the crew were brought to safety. And by now there were plenty of small vessels in the vicinity in case the *Valsesia* should capsize.

As the tide receded the stranded steamer appeared to gain in proportion and the strain of its heavy cargo brought about a most dramatic happening. Suddenly there was a loud report followed by an ominous crashing and crunching noise, which indicated all too plainly that her back was breaking. Rivets flew out from the vessel's plates, she was quite literally falling apart at the seams. The most urgent necessity was to discharge the cargo into lighters as it seemed most unlikely that the *Valsesia* would ever be re-floated – indeed she later split in two. Throughout the month of September several attempts were made to move the two parts but despite the combined efforts of three tugs she remained firmly embedded on the rocks. The wrecked vessel had become an integral part of the Island's attractions – a scene to be visited, photographed and talked

The wreck of the *Valsesia*, firmly embedded in the rocks, finally split in two and became a target for 20th century 'wreckers'.

about. It was not until late October that the salvage company managed to remove the remains and they were scuttled out in Whitemore Bay.

During the later days of August some of the *Valsesia*'s cargo was exposed for several hours during low tides. It would appear that an undisclosed number of persons with horses and carts risked the inherent dangers of the wrecked vessel to cart away some of the coal. It was estimated that over 100 tons was taken though the real figure could have been far greater. Those who were caught suffered fines varying from five shillings to ten shillings depending on the gravity of their crime. The local magistrates made it quite clear that they considered such actions as criminal, but it was an indication just how deeply the four month old coal strike had affected the local community.

Just nine years later Friars Point was once again the scene of a shipping accident and the Barry Island holidaymakers were treated to another dramatic and spectacular 'beach entertainment'. On 17th September 1935 there was a very strong north-west gale blowing along the length of the Bristol Channel with particularly heavy seas pounding the Glamorgan coast. The French schooner *Goeland* was bound from Roscoff to Swansea with a cargo of onions. Most of her sails were torn and tattered from the battering she had received during her journey across the Channel from Lundy. The *Goeland* was driven right across Swansea Bay, making it impossible to shelter in Mumbles Roads. The master and owner, Yves Kerbel, decided to run before the wind in the hope of making Cardiff. She was just about three miles off the coast at Rhoose when the cargo and sand ballast shifted dangerously and caused her to list heavily to port. It was now almost impossible for Captain Kerbel to keep the *Goeland* on course.

Within minutes the captain's problems had multiplied. The constant rolling and the continual heavy seas crashing over the decks caused the boom to break, smashing the wheel and in the process badly injuring the captain about the head and face. More of the rigging collapsed and the thought uppermost in the captain's mind was pure survival for himself and his crew of six. Distress signals were launched and he tried to steer his vessel into the beach at Porthkerry but to no avail. The *Goeland* was being driven relentlessly forward by the force of the gale.

The distress signals were spotted by a Rhoose farmer and his daughter, who immediately notified their nearby Coastguard station. The alarm was raised and passed to the Barry lifeboat station, the message timed at 10.15 in the morning. Although the Barry coxswain was absent, the secretary of the station, Mr A. C. Jones, a retired dock pilot, mustered the crew and took command of the lifeboat himself. The *Prince David* was launched within seven minutes of receipt of the Coastguard message – an amazingly speedy action. It was about a two mile journey to Friars Point, which had to be made directly into the fierce gale. According to an observer the *Prince David* frequently disappeared into deep troughs only to emerge seconds later 'amidst crashing waves and spumes of surf and spray, it was a most dramatic, exhilarating but frightening scene.' The lifeboat took about 25 minutes to close with the stricken vessel.

By now the *Goeland* was in desperate straits, lying almost on her beam ends and surrounded by the debris of sails, rigging and timber. One of her crew was forced to leap overboard in order to get clear of the mass of wreckage on the deck in which he had become entangled. To pick him up the coxswain was made to change course and go broadside into the weather, which almost capsized the lifeboat. Once the man was recovered, the acting coxswain bravely took the lifeboat right alongside the *Goeland* despite the mass of drifting wreckage around the vessel – a calculated risk to the safety of the lifeboat in such a confused and angry sea. The injured captain and the four remaining crew members, who included two boys aged twelve and 14 years, slid down the side of the ship into the water and they were all quickly and expertly hauled aboard the lifeboat. Just as the last survivor was being saved, the *Goeland* struck the rocks. The rescued crew were taken to the Barry pilot lodge where they were fed and clothed by the Shipwrecked Mariners Society.

The badly holed vessel remained on Friars Point for another week, proving to be a most popular sight for hundreds of day-trippers. It was finally bought by a salvage company. There are two happier outcomes of the disaster. The Royal National Lifeboat Institution awarded medals to all the Barry lifeboat crew for 'this dangerous rescue carried out with dash and skill.' Mr Jones received a silver and the other seven members were each awarded a bronze medal. Since the opening of the station in 1901 the *Goeland* rescue was the most outstanding service in its history. There is still a lifeboat stationed at the port. Mr Jenkin Lougher and his daughter, who first raised the alarm, received a letter of appreciation from the French Consul at Cardiff.

On reflection it was fully recognised that the alacrity with which the alarm was raised and the speed of response by the lifeboat crew was crucial in saving the six lives; a delay of only a few minutes could have proved fatal. Be that as it may, the two tales of the wrecks on Barry Sands were told and re-told in Cardiff and the valleys by those who had spent a day out by the 'holiday sea'.

'A Watery Grave
By Day Or Night'

Lundy is a small island, some three miles long and half a mile wide, situated eleven miles north-west of Hartland Point off the north Devon coast. This steep granite plateau runs almost due north to south and stands as a sentinel to the Bristol Channel, exposed to the full fury of the Atlantic Ocean. All around the island are dramatic cliff faces, some up to 400 ft high, and along its coast are a number of small islands, rocks and submerged reefs making its waters most hazardous to shipping. The full splendour of its dramatic scenery has been best captured by Charles Kingsley, who visited Lundy in 1849. He set the tragic final scene of *Westward Ho* at the Shutter Rock in the south-east corner of the island:

> '. . . On their left hand as they broached to, the wall of granite sloped down from the clouds towards an isolated peak of rock, some two hundred feet in height. Then a hundred yards of roaring breaker upon a sudden shelf, across which the race of the tide poured like a cataract; then, amid a column of salt smoke, the shutter, like a huge black fang, arose waiting for its prey . . .'

The island has a long, chequered but fascinating history, being used at various times as a base by Vikings, pirates and smugglers, and is now owned by the National Trust. It has long been known as a danger to shipping; back in 1786 the Bristol merchants maintained that it took 'a great toll of shipping'. This was especially so in the 19th century when it was estimated that no less than 80,000 vessels passed the island annually and on many days 300 ships were within sight at one time, with perhaps 150 vessels at anchor in the Roads to the sheltered east of the island. With such a magnitude of shipping traffic and Lundy's quickly changing weather, it is perhaps not surprising that there were many wrecks not only along its coasts but also in the waters around the island. It has been estimated that well over 180 vessels were wrecked there between the years 1811 to 1950 and the Marisco Tavern, the island's only inn, has its walls liberally decorated with items salvaged from the many wrecks over the years.

The earliest recorded wreck was the collier *Marie*, which became stranded on 19th September 1757 with a total loss of life. However, there is no doubt that there were very many earlier wrecks and indeed numerous unrecorded wrecks later, but because Lundy was so isolated and for long periods in the 18th century was a stronghold of smuggling gangs, very little information filtered out.

Because of the rugged nature of its coast there was a considerable loss of life in several of the wrecks; in 1904 it was estimated that in October 1886 over 300 lives were lost 'inside Lundy' from the 18 to 20 steamers that foundered. During the terrible storm of 24/25th October 1859, which has passed into history as the 'Great Royal Charter Gale', no less than seven vessels went down with a total loss of life. According to an islander, 'the only bodies we recovered were those of four foreigners and their bodies were buried in the churchyard'. In February 1877 the iron-built steamer *Ethel* loaded with iron-ore for Cardiff came to grief on Black Rock just off the south-east corner of the island. She struck the rocks in dense fog, 19 of the crew were drowned and only the mate survived. He managed to struggle ashore, climb an almost sheer cliff face and arrive completely exhausted at Millcombe House, the home of the Heaven family, who were for a long time the owners of Lundy. Just ten years later – in March – the *City of Exeter*, a large steamship carrying coal from Cardiff to St Nazaire, foundered in a force ten gale just four miles south-west of the island, when 16 out of a crew of 19 were drowned.

Perhaps one of the unluckiest accidents happened to the crew of the *Llanisley*, a schooner on a voyage from Neath to Penzance with coal. She foundered on 2nd October 1895 in a fierce storm. The crew of four abandoned their vessel just south of Lundy, took to the 'ship's punt' and made for Ilfracombe. When they were in sight of the shore, the punt capsized in the surf and all four were drowned. Even coming to more recent times, in October 1942, a Dutch motor cruiser *Atlas* became stranded near the Shutters reef and only the mate survived out of a crew of nine.

One of the features of the wrecks on Lundy was the assistance given to the survivors. In the mid 19th century there were about 240 inhabitants, many of them working in the granite quarries. The first lighthouse was established in 1820 at Beacon Hill, the highest point of the island. In 1897 it was replaced by one at the north of the island and another at the south end. One very notable rescue was made in February 1892 when the French vessel *Tunisie* went ashore near Sugar Loaf at the south-east corner. There was a strong north-easterly gale raging, a blinding snow storm and very heavy seas but despite these wretched conditions the lighthouse keeper with seven helpers managed to save all 21 crew members. He adapted a fog signal rocket and a coal bag as an improvised breeches buoy. Largely as a result of this rescue Lundy was first provided with a rocket apparatus in the following year.

The *North Devon Journal* provides a vivid account of the wreck of the *Hannah Moore* on Rat Island in the south-east corner of Lundy on 10th January 1866. The vessel, 1,129 tons, had arrived in Lundy Roads two days previously with a cargo of guano from Chile for Queenstown in Ireland, so she was well off course and had obviously made for Lundy to shelter from the storm, which according to the newspaper report was at least hurricane force. It would appear that the captain attempted to set the sails to beat offshore but they were blown to ribbons by the ferocious winds. The *Hannah Moore* began to drag her anchors, one cable parted and the ship went broadside to the seas, the decks were swept clear of everything and the topmasts collapsed. On the following morning:

'... those on shore saw the crew clinging to the lower rigging. A rescue was organised by a young surgeon on a visit to the island. Two Bideford men, Thomas Saunders and Samuel Jarmon, went out in Mr Heaven's punt and made two attempts to take out a line ... A giant wave lifted the ship onto Rat Island on her side and in twenty minutes she had disintegrated. All but six of the crew were washed off, but those remained on a portion of the wreck from daylight until 4 p.m. After five attempts to reach them in the small punt they were at length brought back to the beach. The remainder were seen clinging to spars and were carried by the eddy round Rat Island to the westward, where they drifted for hours to and fro in the currents before many of them were dashed against the rocks.'

Nineteen of the crew were drowned in this tragic disaster.

Certainly the most spectacular wreck ever in the Bristol Channel occurred on Lundy on 30th May 1906. HMS *Montagu*, a first class battleship of 14,000 tons, struck a point just to the north of Great Shutter Rock in the early hours of the morning when there was a thick fog enveloping the coast of the island. Amazingly not a single member of the crew of 750 officers and men was lost.

The battleship had been built in 1901 at the cost of £1 million and it was one of the six Hunter class vessels all named after admirals. She was fully fitted with the latest technology and was testing her radio apparatus in the Bristol Channel. After she struck the rocks, the vessel listed heavily to starboard. Both propellers were sheered away and she was holed so badly that several compartments flooded. As soon as news of the disaster reached the Admiralty, four battleships and a cruiser were dispatched to the scene and two Liverpool salvage tugs were ordered to Lundy.

Within two days work had started on the removal of much of the valuable equipment, in the hope of lightening the vessel so that she could be re-floated. However, the story of the accident almost reaches the stage of farce. There were considerable disagreements between the Navy and the civilian salvage contractors. One of the lighters which was loaded with four salvaged six-inch guns sank at the Rattles – quite a setback!

It was felt that the *Montagu* could be re-floated on the spring tides later in the month but, by late August, she was still stuck on the rocks. When a steam salvage tug arrived and it was finally agreed that the vessel was a total wreck, the mammoth task of removing all the equipment, including the massive

101

twelve-inch guns weighing 48 tons a piece, began in earnest. The contractors built a rope suspension bridge from the island to the *Montagu* to facilitate the movement of the salvage workers, all of whom lived on the island. A path was dug down from a cliff to the bridge of the vessel and concrete steps constructed, which became known as the 'Montagu Steps'. In 1907 she was sold for salvage and operations continued off and on for the next 15 years. Indeed so famous was the wreck that the Bristol Channel pleasure steamers included it on their regular excursion tours!

The official report of the wreck adds a little humour. It seems that after the accident an officer and a small party landed on the island and started to walk north. The captain was convinced that the vessel had gone aground at or near Hartland Point. So when the officer arrived at the lighthouse at the north of Lundy 'words passed' between him and the lighthouse keeper, until the latter assured him that he really knew which lighthouse he was in charge of! At the court martial the captain and the navigating officer were severely reprimanded and both dismissed their vessel.

Since 1906 there have been many more wrecks on Lundy but fortunately very few in the last 20 years. One very fortunate vessel was the *Maria Kyriakides*, a Greek steamship that went aground at the Quarries (on the east coast) in March 1929. All of the 18 crew were saved and about 18 months later she was successfully re-floated and towed into Ilfracombe – one of the few not to find a watery grave.

'Valour and Virtue'

Since the foundation of the Royal National Lifeboat Institution in 1824, the sea has claimed the lives of no less than 435 lifeboatmen, and 18 from the Mumbles lifeboat station appear on this tragic roll of honour; no other lifeboat station in the Bristol Channel has suffered so grievously. The stirring words of Sir Winston Churchill can be applied to all the gallant and memorable rescues in the Bristol Channel:

'The lifeboat drives on with a mercy, which does not quail in the presence of death, it drives on as a proof, a symbol, a testimony that man is created in the image of God, and that valour and virtue have not perished in the British race.'

The three disasters that have befallen the Mumbles lifeboat occurred in 1883, in February 1903 when the coxswain and five crewmen were drowned and in April 1947. Such tragedies live long in the memories of local communities because often the lifeboat is at the very heart of a town or village, and Mumbles is no exception.

During the afternoon of 23rd April 1947 the *Samtampa*, a large British steamship, was being severely buffeted before a force nine westerly gale. The vessel, an ex-Liberty ship, was bound from Middlesbrough to Newport in ballast. Liberty ships were mass produced, pre-fabricated vessels with all-welded hulls rapidly built in the United States between 1941–5 to replace the shipping tonnage lost during the Second World War. On arrival in Swansea Bay she developed engine trouble and the captain, H. Sherwell, decided to drop anchor in order to sort out the problem. Since the late morning the weather had been worsening by the hour and just after half past four the starboard cable parted, followed 20 minutes later by the port cable.

The remains of the *Samtampa* wrecked, with all lives lost, off Sker Point in April, 1947. (Picture: South Wales Evening Post)

The *Samtampa*, over 7,000 tons, was very high in the water, being in ballast, and she was driven eastwards by the tremendous winds, which were said to be touching hurricane force. At ten minutes to six she sent out a message that she 'was rapidly drifting towards Nash Shoal'. This message was passed on to the Mumbles lifeboat station and at twelve minutes past six the lifeboat *Edward, Prince of Wales* was launched with William Gammon, who had been coxswain for over seven years, at the helm.

After the lifeboat had been launched, the Coastguard received a further message from the distressed vessel giving her precise position, bearing and that she was 'two and a half miles from Porthcawl light'. This information was signalled to the lifeboat but there was no acknowledgement and just about seven o'clock the lifeboat returned for further information. On being given the *Samtampa's* last known position the lifeboat set out for a second time. She was last seen heading across Swansea Bay in a south-easterly direction before being lost to view in the tremendous seas.

The final message from the *Samtampa* was transmitted at just about the same time as the lifeboat set out for the second time:

'To all stations. Starboard anchors carried away. Now drifting ashore. Stand by.'

The *Samtampa* went aground on the rocks just off Sker Point and began to break almost immediately. With 40 or so minutes of continual pounding by the heavy seas, she was soon a complete wreck. The Porthcawl Life Saving Company's rocket apparatus was brought to the beach with great difficulty but such was the ferocity of the weather that it proved impossible to get a line aboard, indeed some of the rockets were blown so far back that they landed on fields way behind the operators. Eyewitness reports suggest that the wrecked vessel was a horrifying sight, 'The huge freighter was being tossed about like a cork, the storm was of an intensity rare in the Bristol Channel.' But of the Mumbles lifeboat there was no sign!

Early in the following morning, when the weather had somewhat moderated, the police were able to board the wreck, now in three pieces, but not one of the crew of 31 had survived. The capsized lifeboat was discovered some 450 yards to the leeside of the wreck; its crew of eight had all perished. The lifeboat was examined by technical experts from the RNLI and they concluded that she had capsized at about high water and had driven over submerged rocks, where she remained fast as the tide ebbed. After the examination the lifeboat was set on fire as is the tradition of the lifeboat service.

The crew of the *Samtampa* were buried in Porthcawl cemetery. The funeral for the lifeboatmen was held on 29th April and they were buried in the churchyard overlooking Mumbles. The day was very wet, torrential rain fell on the cortege as it made its slow way along the crowded narrow streets of the village. The tragedy deeply affected the nation and contributions to the fund for dependents were received from all parts of the country. The replacement lifeboat arrived on station in late July and by common agreement was named *William Gammon* as a mark of respect to the coxswain and as a lasting memorial to him and his crew.

Aground in the Avon Gorge

The port of Bristol is situated some seven miles from the Bristol Channel and is reached by a long and tortuous journey up a muddy and treacherous river. In places the mudbanks are steep and the twists and turns of the river Avon make navigation a special problem. In the days of sailing ships the steep cliffs of the Avon Gorge often left a vessel without any wind, thus increasing the dangerous nature of this busy waterway. It must be said that the river gives Bristol surely the most splendid approach to any port in the world, but given these natural hazards combined with a high tidal range (some 36 ft between high and low) it is not surprising that many ships became stranded high and dry along the banks of the Avon.

On Sunday morning, 12th May 1878, the schooner *Gipsy* became stranded in the Avon Gorge and effectively blocked the river passage to all but the smallest vessels, bringing the port of Bristol to a virtual standstill.

The *Gipsy* was a regular visitor to the port. She belonged to the Waterford Steam Navigation Company and operated on a cargo and passenger service between Bristol, Liverpool and Waterford. The *Gipsy* had arrived in the port with a cargo of livestock and some passengers. After unloading and then loading a general cargo she left just after midnight – a very quick turn-round considering she had only docked early on Saturday morning. The tide was full and she was being towed by the tug *Sea King*. The two passed under the Clifton Suspension Bridge at about three o'clock in the morning and when she reached a point known as 'Black Rock', the *Gipsy* struck the rock and mud on the Bristol bank. Fortunately her bow was only a few feet from the shore and the one passenger on board was quickly

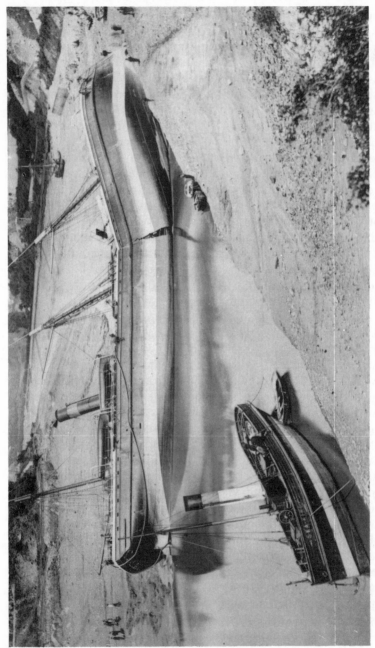

The wreck of the *Gypsy* in the river Avon, May 1878, blocking all traffic to and from the Port of Bristol. (Picture: Reece Winstone Archive)

helped to safety, followed by the crew. She listed over to one side and entirely blocked the river.

When the news of the stranding spread to the port, people in their hordes came to view the disaster. By the afternoon when tugs tried to move the stranded ship, the crowds were said to be 'in their thousands'. Many had swarmed onto the Avonmouth railway line, which afforded the best view. According to the local press 'loud shriekings from approaching engines were necessary to warn the public of their danger'. The spectators were given a wonderful free 'entertainment', if such a term could be used. When the tugs failed to move the vessel, a steam fire engine was brought by open barge to pump out the water before the crew could start unloading the cargo. Then at about eight o'clock in the evening 'there was a loud report like the discharge of a cannon, caused by the steamer parting in two, or, as it is familiarly known, breaking her back. Immediately upon this the men made a rush to leave the steamer but it soon became known that there was no real danger and they remained on board and pursued their task.'

It was decided to use dynamite to remove the *Gipsy* and an expert from Glasgow was called in to supervise the operation. Even by mid-week the vessel and its demolition was still causing intense public interest. Although there had been 'an unusually heavy downfall of rain', thousands of spectators tramped through nearly three-quarters of a mile of mud 'varying in depth from a half to one and a half feet but notwithstanding this somewhat unpleasant drawback, there seemed yesterday (14th May) to be more feminine than masculine visitors to see what was going on at the scene of the disaster.' This was a veritable hive of activity, with 500 labourers engaged in taking the *Gipsy* apart and over 100 'navvies' widening the river channel by removing the bank on the opposite side of the river.

By Thursday (16th) part of the river channel was open to small craft and then on the following day several large vessels were able to pass up to the port, but it would be several weeks before the channel was completely free. The last charge of dynamite was laid on 4th June and a young lad was injured by flying metal, though he was standing some 400 yards away from the scene. Even three weeks after the accident there were still plenty of onlookers, indeed the locals hadn't been afforded such a long-running free spectacle for a long time and no doubt, Captain Parsons, the Havenmaster and the Dock Committee hoped that another would not happen again, at least during their term of office!

It would be another 51 years before a similar disaster struck the port and this one proved to be even more spectacular. On 1st November 1929 during a dense fog no less than seven vessels of various sizes were stranded in the river. Two large steamships, *Bristol City* and *Sappho*, had left Bristol docks and at the same time and on the same tide, the *Peursam* and the *New York City* were coming up the river to Bristol. The thick fog suddenly came down, reducing visibility to barely a couple of feet. The various masters and pilots were helpless, incapable of guiding their vessels. It was said that all that could be heard was the frantic and shrill sounds of the ships' sirens and the ominous and loud crunching noises as vessels hit one another before becoming stranded on the mud-banks.

SS *Bristol City* stranded in the Avon, November 1929. (Picture: Reece Winstone Archive)

As the tide started to ebb the full enormity of the scale of the disaster could be seen. The *Bristol City* had virtually turned full circle and her bows were pointing back along the river from whence she had come. The *Peursam* had grounded close by and as the tide receded she slipped slowly down the mud to come to rest finally on the *Bristol City*. The other Bristol City Line steamship, the *New York City*, had been stranded slightly higher up the river and although her rudder was put out of action, she was re-floated on the next tide and towed back to Avonmouth. All the vessels were moved and within 24 hours the river channel was opened again to shipping. By some miracle not one life was lost on any of the stranded vessels or on the numerous salvage tugs that came to assist. However, one of the thousands of spectators fell into the river and drowned before he could be rescued.

The river Avon is now a relative back-water compared with the heyday of the port so it is highly unlikely that any such 'traffic jam' will happen again.

Threepence A Look!

Equinoctial gales are not uncommon features of the weather pattern of Wales and the West Country and when they arrive they are well-known for their intensity, frequently more severe than winter storms. But the gale that raged along the south Glamorgan coast during 15th and 16th October 1886 was particularly extreme; it left in its wake a trail of devastation and death both on land and at sea. It also managed to tarnish indirectly the reputation of those living along the coast from Porthcawl to Nash Point.

The first vessel to fall foul of the execrable weather was the *Ben-y-Gloe*, a large sailing ship, which was bound for Penarth from Singapore with a cargo of timber and rubber. The master, Captain Gill, and his crew had striven manfully to bring the badly storm-damaged vessel along the Welsh coast, despite being continually battered by very heavy seas throughout her passage up the Bristol Channel. When she was close to Nash Point she heeled over but the crew endeavoured to save themselves by taking to the rigging. Just after midnight on the 15th the vessel became grounded near Nash Sands, and as the tide ebbed the crew managed to scramble ashore safely. Most of them were said to be almost naked because the wind had been so fierce that their clothes had been stripped from their backs.

Exhausted and suffering from exposure their first thought on reaching safety was to find some shelter, food and rest. They stumbled inland to the nearest village – Marcross – just a mile or so from the coast. They knocked at the local inn, where, by all accounts, the innkeeper only allowed them into one of his storerooms, where they were forced to lie down on a stone floor in what was left of their sodden and ragged clothes; there was no fire nor the offer of any dry clothes. The innkeeper refused to provide any food or drink because they had no money to pay.

Captain Gill, who was the last to leave the vessel, finally arrived at the inn at about 2.30 in the morning and demanded food for himself and his crew. The innkeeper still wanted to see the colour of their money but he was given short shrift from Captain Gill, who told him in no uncertain manner that the money would be paid. It was six o'clock before any hot food and drinks were provided.

As if this ungracious and hostile reception was not enough for the stranded crew to suffer, when they returned to their vessel the following morning to pick up their belongings, they found to their dismay and horror that in the meantime she had been plundered and most of their possessions had been stolen. The captain maintained that they had been deliberately misled by the locals, who had assured them that the tide was rising and that they should save their lives while they could. This, he felt, was a deliberate ruse to get rid of them so that the locals could concentrate on their looting.

The police reported that people for miles around had come to plunder the wreck, 'like bees around a honey jar'. Despite a very thorough search few goods were recovered, though some were found under a chapel pulpit in a neighbouring village. There was a local tramp, who had obtained so much from the stranded ship that henceforth he was nicknamed 'Benny Gloe'!

The newspapers throughout South Wales were forceful in their universal condemnation of the looting of the vessel and the churlish attitude to 'these poor unfortunate sailors'. Those responsible for such 'inhuman behaviour' were labelled as 'wretches that have besmirched the reputation and honour of all Welsh people, they acted in a most callous and ruthless manner, without a care or thought for the plight and suffering of their fellow humans.' These comments were somewhat influenced by what happened in the aftermath of the second shipwreck on that fateful day.

The *Malleny* was an iron-built sailing vessel, which had left Cardiff a day earlier fully loaded with a cargo of coal for Rio de Janiero. She was towed to some miles west of Lundy and when the tug left, the captain's problems started. The wind had increased appreciably in strength and he decided to return to

Swansea Bay for shelter. The *Malleny* staggered back and it was while she was crossing the bay that she was battered by particularly heavy seas, which put her rudder out of action and left the vessel effectively out of control. Soon she was being driven back across the bay, drifting closer and closer inshore. The *Malleny* was sighted from the land in obviously a most distressed condition but because the storm had brought the telegraph lines down, no message could be sent to alert the Porthcawl lifeboat station. By now the *Malleny* was sending up distress rockets, before she struck Tusker Rock. The crew of 20 men were all drowned and she finally went ashore at Westward Ho, right across the other side of the Channel.

Most of the crew were coloured, indeed the captain's small daughter was found in the arms of one of the coloured seamen. Four of the bodies were collected from the shore by cart and were deposited at the Greyhound Inn, St Brides Major. During the evening the publican put the four bodies on public display and charged threepence a look – such was the rarity value of coloured men in those parts. The innkeeper was later charged with obtaining money by false pretences, though he claimed that the 'admission fee' was to help defray the cost of burial! The defendant was discharged on the judge's advice, who commented that if perverted persons were prepared to pay hard-earned money for such 'a macabre peepshow' that this was not a crime against any laws of the land but 'a crime against human dignity and mankind'.

Much of the public censure was not directed at the innkeeper but rather towards the coxswain and the crew of the Porthcawl lifeboat. The coxswain defended his decision not to launch the boat by maintaining that 'even a tug wouldn't have gone out in such a storm. If it had, the lives of the crew would have been sacrificed.' Nevertheless, the foreman of the inquest jury commented, 'Porthcawl must be a bad place to keep a lifeboat if she can't go out in rough weather.' This criticism of the Porthcawl lifeboat crew was not only harsh but most unjustified. The lifeboat, the *Chafyn Grove*, which had been provided by a Miss Chafyn Grove of Zeals in Wiltshire, had been on the station since 1872. In just three years it had made three notable rescues. In April 1881 it had rescued eight men off the Danish barque *Marmora*, which shortly after became a total wreck. Then in the following March eight out of a crew of eleven were rescued from the French steamer *Liban*, which sank on the Tusker Sands. During a severe north-west gale in August 1883 the lifeboat went out in the very rough seas to assist the barque *William Miles*, which was breaking up and sinking just a mile from Porthcawl harbour. It only managed to take off the master's wife and one man because of the heavy swell. Although the weather worsened the lifeboat made a second trip and this time managed to recover the master and the rest of the crew. To pontificate from the warmth and security of a court-room showed a sad lack of appreciation of the dangers and hardships faced by lifeboatmen.

The local newspapers were full of condemnation of the 'wicked peepshow' and, coming so close in time to the other happenings just a couple of miles along the coast, they express-ed grave disquiet at the callous and rapacious attitude of the people living in the area. However, they did manage to lighten the gloom with at least one happy story. The carpenter on the *Malleny*, Edwin Waters, had been paid off from the vessel when she was in Amsterdam in early September. His family in Apple-dore were not aware of this fact, all they knew was that the ship had been lost with all hands. When the fortunate Waters finally arrived back he found all his relations wearing black in mourn-ing for his 'death'.

This rather lovely stretch of coast, now a Heritage Coast, took a long time to live down the sad and sorry happenings of 15th October 1886.

The Iron-Bound Coast

Of all the splendid scenery that is to be found along both sides of the Bristol Channel, none can surpass for sheer grandeur the high and lofty stretch of coast which runs south from Hartland Point to Morwenstow. The massive soaring cliffs fall steeply, at places vertically, to the water's edge, where the pounding ocean and the roar of the wind make this coast so exhilarating and so unforgettable. From these majestic heights the views are truly spectacular; to the south the long sweep of the Cornish coastline, to the north the 'noble walls of Devon', while out to sea Lundy may be seen floating on the waves.

Under a summer sun the coast appears a serene and almost benign seascape but come autumn and winter it assumes a grim, fierce and threatening character, battered by the frequent westerly gales and the full fury of the Atlantic Ocean. This coast has long proved to be a ship's graveyard – no less than 136 in the last 200 years. A traveller in 1895 remarked that there was not 'any half-mile free from the debris of ships that have ended their last voyage on this iron-bound coast'.

Just five years earlier, in December, the *Uppingham* outward bound from Cardiff to China struck the rocks at Long Peak, a formidable and bleak promontory some 400 ft high with a mass of jagged boulders at its base. Of a crew of 28, only ten survived the ordeal. In 1900 the *Welbury* heading for Cardiff struck the same rocks barely a couple of yards from where the *Uppingham* had stranded. By that strange coincidence which often happens at sea, the second officer on the *Welbury* had previously survived the earlier wreck!

Perhaps the most celebrated wreck along this coast in recent years has been the *Green Ranger*, which came to grief on the

116

Long Peak in 1962. It was during the afternoon of 17th November, as the 3,000 ton Fleet Auxiliary tanker was being towed by the tug *Caswell* for a re-fit at Cardiff. The two vessels were caught in a most severe north-easterly gale and late in the afternoon the tow-line parted in mountainous seas just off Hartland Point. The *Green Ranger* with her small retaining crew of seven was left at the mercy of the tremendous seas and the ferocity of the storm, which was blowing directly onto the shore. Soon she was being driven closer and closer to the 'iron-bound coast'.

One of the crew members vividly described the scene:

'Because of the heavy seas and the strong wind, we were just not making any headway and about 4.15 p.m. we lost contact with the tug. For a couple of hours we drifted helplessly and then we went to ground stern first with a most tremendous bang. The waves were pounding us and as the ship started to list we climbed to the highest point and sat huddled in the darkness. It was nerve-wracking because the ship was a mass of green water and twisting all the time . . .'

All the rescue services in the area were alerted. An RAF helicopter from Chivenor, near Barnstaple, was unable to rescue the crew because of the violent gusting wind, which was said to be up to 70 mph. The Hartland Lifesaving Company were quickly on the scene but because of the force of the wind blowing directly on-shore, the rockets they fired from the cliff-top failed to find the vessel. Both the Clovelly and Appledore lifeboats were launched but unfortunately the Clovelly boat could not make any headway against the high seas and the ferocity of the storm. However, the Appledore boat, *Louisa Anne Hawker* commanded by Coxswain Sydney Camm, managed to fight her way across Bideford Bay in what had become a force ten storm.

The lifeboat reached Hartland Point some 75 minutes later and proceeded to search for the stricken vessel. The conditions were atrocious, sleet and hail-storms swept the sea and the visibility was almost nil. After about an hour or so the *Green Ranger* was sighted in the searchlights of HMS *Agincourt*, a destroyer from Milford Haven which had been ordered into the search area. She was listing heavily to port with waves con-

117

The Life Saving Company at work. (Picture: Illustrated London News)

tinually breaking right over her, but there was no sign of the crew.

Coxswain Camm brought the lifeboat right under the tanker's bow and using an anchor and the engines with great skill manoeuvred the boat into a very narrow area of confused and churning water under the lee of the *Green Ranger*, only a few yards from the rocks. With utmost skill he managed to keep the boat there for almost 15 minutes, whilst the lifeboatmen attempted to make contact with the crew by loud hailer. The lifeboat was in very grave danger from both the wrecked vessel and the jagged rocks and it was an incredible feat of seamanship and bravery. As there was no sign of the crew Coxswain Camm extricated his boat from its dangerous position and joined the destroyer a few hundred yards off the shore to stand by should they be needed. It was not until several hours later that a message was received that the crew had been rescued from the shore. Describing the scene later Coxswain Camm said:

'... At times we were only twelve feet away from the tanker. Then the seas would break against her and our boat would sheer away towards the rocks. We were just missing them. Sometimes we were only four or five feet away ... and every minute we stayed there we might have crashed on the rocks ...'

The scene on shore was equally frightening, where the members of the Lifesaving Company could barely stand against the fierce gusts of wind. When they failed to make contact with their first two rockets, the decision was made to try to climb down the almost sheer cliff face. Three men volunteered to take with them seven heavy rockets, four lines and a hawser. In normal conditions the descent would have been difficult but in such appalling weather it was perilous, especially as the last section was nigh on vertical. Even when the Company reached the beach, they still had the very dangerous task of getting onto the slippery rocks and fighting against the driving spray. Their first rocket firing was successful and slowly, one by one, the crew were hauled off and then assisted up the 400 ft cliff to safety. The truly amazing rescue had taken no less than 15 hours from start to finish and the Hartland LSA Company were later awarded the coveted Wreck Service Shield.

Coxswain Camm and his lifeboat returned to Appledore, arriving about nine o'clock in the morning. For his part in the attempted rescue he received the silver medal of the RNLI to add to his two bronzes and each member of the crew was given a vellum record of thanks. Coxswain Camm finally retired in March 1965 after no less than 53 years in the Lifeboat Service – almost 32 of them as coxswain. Throughout his long service he epitomised the Service's selfless devotion and dedication to the saving of life at sea.

'Such Dreadful News From The West'

There are so few reports of shipwrecks in the 18th century that one might be forgiven for concluding that they were far less prevalent than in the following century. This indeed might be true though there is insufficient contemporary evidence to either prove or disprove such a theory. Many stretches of the Bristol Channel were so isolated in the 18th century that often ships were wrecked and went unreported and unknown other than to the local community. In the 19th century there were many more sources of contemporary information – local newspapers, Customs, Coastguard and lifeboat records and published books; also from 1850 there was an annual register maintained of all shipwrecks in the Kingdom.

The 18th century was barely three years old when one of the worst storms ever to strike the coast of Britain occurred during November 16th and 17th, 1703. Daniel Defoe recorded the disastrous effects of the 'Great Storm', and maintained that over 150 vessels were wrecked and nearly 8,000 lives were lost throughout the country during the two tragic days.

At King Road at the entrance to the river Avon, which had for centuries been the safe anchorage for vessels waiting for the tide, the storm of 1703 was most destructive. The *Richard and John*, which had arrived from Virginia with tobacco, along with a prize vessel *Bandera* were both lost with all hands. Six other vessels at anchor were driven ashore, some quite badly damaged, and it was reported that the Naval vessels *Arundel*, *Suffolk* and *Matthew* were stranded 'high up on the green grass and were got off only with great difficulty.'

In March 1705 there was what was described as a 'calamitous storm' in King Road and two Customs boats foundered. Twenty-two Customs boatmen were drowned in this singular disaster, nearly one third of the total Customs staff at the port of Bristol. Each widow received an annual pension of £7 10s and £1 10s for each child and there were no less than 70 children left fatherless, including 'one motherless daughter aged eight years', who was considered as 'a widow for pension purposes'. Such a bland and matter-of-fact report highlights the human tragedy to be found in most shipwreck stories.

The two most disastrous shipwrecks of the century both concerned Naval vessels, indeed as far as the numbers drowned they were among the most tragic accidents in the whole of the Bristol Channel. The first shipping accident occurred along the Gower Coast and the loss of life was horrific. On 28th November 1760 the Admiralty tender *Caesar* was lying at anchor in Mumbles Roads along with a small tender *Reeves*. The two Naval vessels were patrolling the area for a set purpose – the impressment of able-bodied men into the Navy or in other words the dreaded Press Gang. The *Caesar* set sail on the

A Navel vessel scudding before the wind. From Serres's *Liber Nauticus*.

evening tide, reported to be heading for Carmarthen Bay to try its luck in the numerous small ports. The weather worsened quite quickly and the captain instructed his pilot to return to the relative safety of Mumbles. However, a serious navigational error was made by the pilot, he mistook Pwlldu Head (the highest headland on the Gower) for Mumbles Head and set a course accordingly. The captain took soundings of the depth but within minutes the sound of the waves breaking upon rocks was distinctly heard. Although the leadsman had shouted a warning the vessel could not be brought round and she was driven hard onto the rocks under the headland.

Some of the crew managed to stagger ashore and climb the steep cliff to safety. During the night the vessel broke up and bodies, wreckage and a large quantity of firearms were strewn along the shore. The poor impressed men had been locked in the holds and they had stood virtually no chance of survival. The captain, Adam Drake, later affirmed that no less than 68 of them died in the wreck, indeed he was later asked to contribute to the cost of their burial. The bodies were said to have been interred in one large unmarked grave on the eastern slope of the headland, which today is still known as Gravesend.

Sker Point, a mile or so north-west of Porthcawl, was the scene of the 'Dreadful News from the West', reported as far away as Essex. A Dutch West Indian vessel *Planters Welvard* was homeward bound from Surinam with a cargo of tea, spices and timber. The captain had made a gross error of navigation – he firmly believed that he was sailing up the English Channel. A report in the *Chelmsford and Colchester Gazette* records that all of the crew were drowned and they included three young brothers, who were returning home for their schooling; all the bodies were buried in Newton Nottage churchyard. The report further stated that much of the cargo 'was stolen by the country people, who have no fear of the authorities. Such dire happenings are a common phenomenon along that coast'.

The last year of the century saw the most calamitous shipwreck ever to occur in the Bristol Channel. On 10th February 1799 a Naval sloop-of-war HMS *Weazle* was in Appledore loading up provisions prior to a cruise along the north Cornwall coast on anti-privateer duties. A sloop-of-war was a two-masted vessel of up to 250 tons and they were normally commanded by an officer of the rank of commander, with a crew of 100 to 130 and with an armament of ten to 16 carronades. The *Weazle* was under the command of the Hon. Henry Grey, son of Lord Stamford. The vessel left port on the evening tide and no sooner had she cleared Bideford Bar than the weather worsened as a severe north-westerly gale blew up. The commander decided to try to find shelter under the lee of Baggy Point – the prominent headland north of Braunton Burrows. However, the weather got the better of the vessel and she was driven ashore just a couple of hundred yards short of the Point. It was reported that the whole company of 106 were drowned. Just one body was recovered at the time and that was a woman named Nancy Golding! It was later explained that the woman must have stayed on board after the farewell party at Appledore. Of course it was strictly forbidden for women to remain on board Naval vessels, which were on active service. Her body was buried in Northam churchyard and there is a memorial to her in the church.

The Naval Chronicle for 1799 contains a letter from a Bideford man concerning the tragic accident. Mr John James was writing on 17th February, just five days after the event:

'I heard on Wednesday a funeral sermon for 106 persons unfortunately lost in the *Weazle* on Sunday night. She was in the bay that afternoon, and as the people went to church, the seafaring men felt some anxiety, if the wind should shift a point and blow, which it did. They made every effort to get out to sea, and in vain kept firing signals of distress. It is supposed she got round Baggy Point and struck upon Morte rocks; that fine ship perished and as yet only one body has been taken up, but many are watching from opposite the beach, both yesterday and today, and are fishing up fragments of the wreck. We hear today (Saturday) that the wreck is visible at low water this side of Baggy Point. A sloop that was in distress in the bay on Monday or Tuesday has also gone down, her fate is uncertain. It is expected many bodies will float and be driven on shore the coming spring.'

Index